YOUR MENTAL SPACE

YOUR MENTAL SPACE

A GUIDE TO SCRIPT YOUR DOPAMINE DIARIES AND SEROTONIN STORIES

ARJUN KARTHIK

PAPER TOWNS
PUBLISHERS

PAPER TOWNS
PUBLISHERS

First published by
Papertowns Publishers
72, Vishwanath Dham Colony,
Niwaru Road, Jhotwara,
Jaipur, 302012

ISBN Print Book - 978-81-947125-6-5

For my Dad, Mom, Sister
and
all the good loving souls

CONTENTS

PART THREE
HACKS

Introduction

Life is a game. All that is necessary is knowing how to play. Success and failures are all part and parcel of the game. There will be people who praise you and there will be people who will talk ill of you behind your back. You must know how to handle them and play a safe, enjoyable game.

Have you ever wondered how beautiful the world around you is? Life is given to you to cherish each and every moment of it. Life is to be appreciated and not to be complained about. All that is required is a little bit of fine-tuning to enjoy your life to the fullest. The definition of happiness varies from individual to individual. It depends on their perception and perspective of life. You need to discover your path to be happy, or you have to be happy with whatever way life takes you. Ultimately, it is your choice. Observe every little detail and be consciously aware of everything in your life. Experiment on what makes you happy. Life is a gruelling process of trial and error. Never worry if you fail or something goes wrong. Consider it as a lesson and convince yourself that nothing is permanent and move on. Always plan what you should do well in advance. Don't allow yourself to stay idle. Focus on finding a solution rather than aggravating the problem. Remember, life is not a problem to be solved but a reality to be experienced. Don't take failure to heart and success to your head. Accept the unchangeable and change the changeable.

Be aware of your everyday thoughts and analyse, whether they are leading you to a better life or not. More often than not, our beliefs and negative mindset tends to limit further progress. Replace your negative thoughts with positive ones. We are what we think we are. We are in constant fear of the WHAT IF that occurs and other such outcomes. We fear and worry about unnecessary things; 90 percent of what you fear, never actually happens at all. It is unwise to sabotage yourself by worrying what others might think of you. Live your life only for yourself. Don't give too much power to others nor let them control you. Also, never allow your level of happiness to be determined by others. The way you think and act are determined by external factors which you allow to enter your life. Remember, only if you allow and open the gates for them, will they ever influence and determine your level of happiness. Learn to sit back and observe your life like a movie. Avoid overreacting to unnecessary situations. Remember, not everything requires a reaction. Don't concern yourself with people or situations; both are powerless without your reaction. You deserve to live your life your desired way. It is your life, which you deserve to live to the fullest and enjoy every moment in this universe.

This book is a gentle reminder of your self-worth. The idea behind this book is to transform your self-image forever and to change your life in a better and positive way.

ARJUN KARTHIK

PART ONE

THE USER MANUAL

KNOWING YOURSELF

Knowing yourself is the beginning of all wisdom.
-Aristotle

To know yourself is your foremost priority. Knowing who you are is the basis of living. Knowing yourself in and out is an essential skill, without which life becomes extremely difficult. To read a book, you should know the meaning of the words formed by different combinations of the 26 letters, making it into sentences, and conveying different meanings. The first step of getting on track or a map for your life is first to know yourself completely. In order to achieve this, you must be aware of your strengths, weaknesses, likes, and dislikes. In addition, observe and be aware of your moods, reactions, and responses to the occurrences around you. Become aware of how these moods and emotions affect your state of mind. The way every person handles a situation is different. Years of trial and error can enable you to handle such situations. Discover unique ways of handling situations. You must learn to analyse the outcome of your behaviour and the potential impact it may create on you and others.

To make your life simpler, you have to understand yourself completely. Knowing yourself improves the quality of your life. Furthermore, understanding yourself better, in turn, leads to better decision making, setting and reaching appropriate goals, and ultimately living a productive, meaningful, and good life. If you fail to understand who you are or what you truly want, you will fail to achieve anything in your life. In turn, this leads to not setting a proper goal, which often leads to being lost and hopeless. This predicament is similar to walking in the darkness.

All that is necessary to be done is to maintain a rhythm with life. You can be in sync with life only when you know how your instrument functions. Unless you comprehend the sounds that the strings of your guitar can produce, you can't expect to play it well enough to produce good music.

Likewise, when you know yourself completely, you hold the key to a happy living. If you know your pros and cons, likes and dislikes, things that make you happy or sad, specific reactions to a situation, and the true purpose of your life, it will ignite a spark of alignment within you and will aid you with being in sync with your life.

When a question of "Who are you?" is asked, we generally respond with, "I am a human being" or "I am a part of nature" or "I am a child of God." On further thought, you were merely a spermatozoon successfully fused to an ovum and born after 40 weeks of development inside your mother's womb, which is the entire cycle of birth. Congratulations, this makes you a human being. You were just 2.5 kilograms and now look at you. You've grown up to become a wonderful individual. Your body has become prominent with all the food you had eaten. A cumulation of all your experiences, thoughts, and beliefs has shaped your mind in a certain manner. You are made up of flesh and bones with blood running through your veins. Your brain acts as the master component controlling the body, with itself being controlled by numerous external factors. Some people are angry all the time while others maintain a cool-head. It can be attributed to various factors such as the environment you were brought up in, the people who brought you up, your past experiences, beliefs, the people you were influenced by, and so on. All these factors shaped you to be able to live under the banner of your name. Who you are now, is a cumulation of past experiences.

We usually identify ourselves with our name, religion, caste, nationality, education, and other such identities. We take our identities very seriously as it highlights who you are to society. More often than not, people judge you only by your identity. What you are when no one is watching is the true version of yourself. Thus, what you choose to present to the world is a sugar-coated version of you. We always desire to show off just to maintain our image. It is just an identity, but not your true self. You are not the body, you are not even the mind, you are a SOUL trapped in this body. When you realize this, you will also realize everything is ONE. At the most basic level of reality, everything is one. The distinction among individual things is merely an illusion. In reality, everything is one.

ATMAN AND BRAHMAN

ATMAN refers to an "individual soul." Atman refers to the eternal essence of each living thing, plants, animals, and human beings. The Atman is not the body while the body is not infinite. The body houses the Atman until it eventually dies. Atman is immortal, eternal, and is on par with the highest metaphysical reality of the universe. Seeking liberation through recognizing the illusion of the phenomenal world and acquiring knowledge of one's true identity is defined as Atman.

Brahman is the "cosmic soul.". It is not an individual being. It is the reality of all beings and existence. It is the eternal essence of the universe and the ultimate divine reality. Also, it is the life source of all that has been, is, and will be throughout the entire cosmos.

Furthermore, Brahman is the substance of the universe. Without attachment to self, Atman is Brahman. It is all that exists, which is not something that contains you or something that creates you.

You and the universe you live in are not two different entities. Everything is one. All that you consider as you, me, he, she, it, everything, and everyone are one. It may seem to sound different. However, it is similar to the concept of a tree where we see flowers, leaves, and branches all being different from one another, but identified as a TREE all together. We are all fragmented energy from the same source.

I am other than name, form and action.
My nature is ever free!
I am Self, the supreme unconditioned Brahman.
I am pure Awareness, always non-dual.
—Adi Shankara

BODY, MIND AND SOUL

The Body

The body is the physical aspect of the human being made up of flesh and bones. It consists of millions of cells which organize to form tissues, nerves, bones, and organs. The body can be considered as a vehicle for the soul. It is a complex machine. Without the soul, which is the vital life force, the body is useless. The human body is fascinating and mysterious. Each part is an interesting aspect. Take your hand and observe it a bit deeply; how many small bones, small muscles, nerves are present, and the various functions your hand performs. We write, draw, eat, drive, beat up someone with our hand and do all the minute activities with our hands. The brain constitutes only about 2 percent of the human body. Yet, it controls all core functions of the body, interprets information from the outside world, and embodies the essence of the mind and soul. It weighs approximately only 1400 grams, but it performs thousands of tasks which requires millions of complex mental calculations from different parts of the brain. The brain receives information through our five senses: sight, smell, touch, taste, and hearing. The information received is processed and a stimulus is sent back to your different organs and you respond to it accordingly. The brain controls our thoughts, memory, speech, movement of the arms and legs, and all the functions of our body. Every day this occurs as an automated process without a great deal of effort. For example, you go out for a walk in the park and you meet your friend. Now, your visual perception confirms that you have definitely met this person before and your memory provides you with the ability to make conversations about the last time you had met and respond accordingly. Neurotransmitters like dopamine, serotonin, and adrenaline are chemical messengers that transmit messages and are responsible for how you feel and react. Dopamine and serotonin are associated with happiness and regulating your mood. It may be as simple as getting positive feedback for the photo you had posted on social media or responding to someone whom you punched in the face to maintain your respect in society and to exact revenge. Your brain is constantly regulating your body. Sometimes when you drive, you start from home and you lose track of what happens but manage to reach your office. When you sit in your car, your brain subconsciously controls your speed by analyzing the speed of other cars going on the road, stopping you during the red light, and turning left or right as required to avoid a collision. This just happens automatically. Driving your car requires more effort from the brain. It has different regions that function to keep you alert and responsive. When you are behind the steering wheel, the Frontal lobe acts as your warning apparatus against impending danger as it alerts your reflexes. The Parietal lobe acts as your gauge on how hard you slam the brakes or how far you steer. The Occipital lobe processes everything you see around to know exactly where to steer. Lastly, the Temporal lobe provides you with alertness based on what you hear. All these processes take place inside your brain while you drive spontaneously and automatically. Your body is your vehicle for everything that happens in your life. The whole human experience depends on your body. Thus, it is crucial to take utmost care of your body.

Your body is precious.
It is your vehicle for awakening.
Treat it with care.
-Buddha

The Mind

The mind processes numerous factors, such as thoughts, ideas, feelings, and emotions. It constitutes the thinking aspect of human beings. The mind can be differentiated into two :

The Conscious Mind

Our everyday thoughts and activities which we are aware of consciously are due to the conscious mind. Thinking and reasoning are the primary functions of our conscious mind. Your awareness of yourself and the world around you is a part of your consciousness.

The Subconscious mind

Our beliefs, behaviour, feelings, and emotions are all part of the subconscious mind. We are usually unaware of the subconscious mind. It does not require any conscious effort, but it functions automatically.

Vivid thoughts always occupy the mind. It is the thought process that drives our physical body to experience everything. All our thoughts and beliefs take place within our mind. Your behaviour and actions generate responses like anger, fear, pain, happiness, and sadness. Over time, the mind creates a memory of the experience, which influences your future actions. Your mind starts to make decisions based on prior experiences. This process takes place subconsciously. It is as if you have been programmed subconsciously and once programmed, you believe and act accordingly. Your mind controls everything. Your attitude and your perspectives can be learned, unlearned, programmed, and reprogrammed with a simple change in your mindset.

Mindset is everything

Our mind must be aligned with our soul to make decisions that feel right. We are born to experience life and to fulfil our desires in a way that satisfies our soul. However, life becomes complicated when thoughts flow in a never-ending cycle in your mind. Learn to silence the mind and the soul will speak.

The mind is like water. When it is turbulent,
it is difficult to see. When it is calm,
everything becomes clearer.
-Dalai Lama

The Soul

You don't have a soul.
You are a soul.
You have a body.
- C.S.Lewis

Your soul is the immaterial essence and totality of who you are. It is your true nature. The soul is the non-physical aspect of a human being and is the core of our existence. It resonates with us in silence when we require guidance. The soul is the part of us that is constantly in the pursuit of the true meaning of life and finding answers to mysterious questions such as "Who am I?", "Why am I here?", and "What is my purpose?" The soul is the eternal life force. It guides and directs our behaviour and actions. It is our soul that provides us with a kind of inner voice, a moral compass, and direction. Also, it is our soul that constantly reminds us that there is more we can become, and strives to give our lives meaning and purpose—the body, mind, and soul functions in tandem as an integrated system of energy. If you consider the body as your car, then your soul is the driver. The soul is the eternal and meta-physical subject brimming with consciousness. It has no shape or form. However, it acts as our inner gut feeling and guiding light to discover the true meaning of our life. If life is a dark room, then the soul is the guiding light. This invisible beacon aids us to acknowledge and be aware of our life.

Intuition is seeing with the soul.
— Dean Koontz

Intuition is the phenomenon of bridging the heart and mind through an intangible sense or feeling. It is the ability to acquire knowledge without inference and to understand something instinctively, without the need for conscious or logical reasoning. It is a deep innate guidance system. This can be referred to as your so-called Gut instinct. Currently, people are engaged in hectic schedules and suffer from immense stress. Life progresses so fast that they barely have any time to find peace, tune into their inner self, nor pay attention to their intuition. People are not aware that intuition is our natural connection which leads us in the right direction. Logic directs us in one way, while the soul directs us on the opposite path from time to time. We have detached from our inner guidance system or instinct. We need logic, reasoning, and proof for everything in our life. When this happens, people start to make compromises in life, giving power to what others think they should do rather than what they really want to do. As a result, they fail to attain a feeling of fulfillment and true happiness. Start to recognize and connect with your inner guidance system. Follow your natural blueprint and life path rather than a compromised life directed towards satisfying the standards set by others and pressures created by society. More often than not, we tend to worry about what others may think and relegate ourselves to stay in that status quo. When you allow these negative and useless thoughts to cloud your thoughts, you will hinder your light from shining through. We need to learn to trust the wisdom of nature and follow the guidance that rises from within. Always trust your intuition; it never lies.

Intuition is the whisper of the soul
- J.Krishnamurthi

In the Bhagavad Gita, Krishna tells Arjuna,

That indwelling Self is ever changeless, imperishable, and without limitation. Only these fleshly garments can be destroyed. Weapons cannot cut the soul; fire cannot burn it; water cannot drown it; wind cannot wither it away!

In the absence of a sound mind, body, and soul connection, anything directly affecting an individual in any one of these areas, will affect all other areas as well. When a thought-provoking question of "Who am I?" is ever raised, it should be realized that you are not the body, you are not even the mind; you are a SOUL. When you understand this simple concept, you will start to look at your life from a whole different perspective.

THOUGHT

Thought is the basic foundation of everything. A thought maybe an idea, an image, a sound or even an emotional feeling that arises from the brain. It is a *representation* of something. Our thoughts are maps representing and corresponding to things that our brain has either perceived with our senses, felt with our emotions or formed by our imagination. Our thoughts become our actions. We become what we think. Right from the time you wake up, a river of thoughts flows through your mind regarding past mistakes, imaginary future outcomes, and other fantasies. Explore your thoughts and feelings and attempt to understand why you think that way. Be in control of your thoughts and you will be in control of your life.

How does a thought arise?

When you think a bit deeper and ask yourself; Where do our thoughts come from? What influences our thoughts? In actuality, our thoughts are influenced by what we see, hear, feel, touch, and taste. It is influenced by the books we read, the movies we watch, the music we listen to, and so on. There is no definite conclusion to why does a thought arise. However, the way you think is definitely influenced by what you do and the people around you. Our thoughts create our beliefs, which forms our core values and dictates our behaviour. Sometimes, someone, somewhere, and somehow instilled a thought or belief into us, similar to a software program inside your subconscious mind. Consider a movie as an example. In general, we adore the protagonist but despise the antagonist. It is due to our belief that the protagonist does good and receives praise, while the antagonist indulges in dastardly acts and should be hated. Our brain detects similarities or correspondences between newly and previously encountered situations, enabling the application of previously learned information to the new situation. Our brain forms the image of ourselves, through the lens of what we had internalized from our parents. This sense of self becomes our authentic identity. Once established, we continue to believe it. Our brain actively copies and absorbs the characters of people that we know and meet, while remembering not only their physical characteristics but also their mental character as well. Another peculiar thought is that an individual can seemingly transform from himself into somebody else. This is owing to the thought that, following or imitating said person will enable you to resemble them or become successful like them. As they say; like father like son. Children often look and act in a similar manner to their parents. It is because they generally adapt their characteristics from their father. The period of early childhood is responsible for moulding you into who you become and how you perceive the world around you . When a child is raised well, teaching him/her how to be good will naturally reciprocate.

On the other hand, if he/she is raised in a terrible or abusive environment and, the child will eventually grow to become rude and bad. The way you think and perceive your childhood greatly influences things. Each thought you have is influenced by something in one way or the other. Undoubtedly, we are ruled by our thoughts. They can be compared to commands given to the computer. Even the thought of food can cause salivation and even the thought of losing someone can make you feel worried. Simply stated, our own thoughts program us.

Thoughts are transmitted expressively through speech. We cannot communicate and share our thoughts if the person I wish to converse with speaks only French while I am able to speak only English. My deep thoughts reside inside my bubble of consciousness, while your thoughts are inside yours.

There is no such thing as a magical direct transmission of thoughts from one person to another. Communication is the vehicle that allows my imagination to reach yours, despite our complete separateness. It is possible for me to express my imagination and you to experience it, only if you understand my language. The words I express originate from within me and are transformed with the help of paper and ink. When you read this, you recreate my words in your state of consciousness and are thus able to understand the message I am trying to convey. The process of reading this book is your receptive re-creation from my words.

If the voice in your head is you,
then who's the one listening to it?

When you become aware that the voices in your head are disconnected from you, then you will discover who you truly are. There exists a profound disparity between the voices in your head and your SELF. Observe these voices from the consciousness of the observer and not from a perspective of the mind. Fundamentally, every human being is the same. However, everyone is programmed differently by their thoughts. Comparing a human being to a music player, but different cassettes produce different genres of music in this scenario. The individual can be compared to the music player, while thoughts are the cassettes making music. Without these cassettes, such music would cease to exist.

Similarly, life becomes dull without your thoughts. It is crucial to adjust your relationship with these thoughts running in your head. How we relate to these thoughts and how we reciprocate with it ultimately alters the course of our thinking and life. Being aware of the voices in your head is a part of conscious awakening. When your conscious awareness heightens, you tend to identify yourself with the mind to a lesser extent. You will develop a unique sense of yourself and learn to create a gap of mindfulness between you, and the voices you depend on to identify as "YOU". The voices in your head are completely normal. However, as you progress into a state of consciousness, you will notice a distinct feeling of detachment from you.

You can either choose to alter them or even mute them to a point where your life becomes quiet and serene.

When unnecessary thoughts constantly sway your mind, learn to calm down, channel your inner peace, and enter into a thoughtless state. Remember to take a break for your routine thought process and try to be yourself without the voices in your head; in a state of nothingness and serenity. Eliminate the negative voices in your head and replace them with positive ones. Understanding and changing the voices in your head is an art and is crucial. However, it is still a process of trial and error. When you learn how to handle them, you will be in complete control of your life and you can steer it in the direction you please.

It is the array of thoughts in your mind that rules you. The way you think is the way you live your life and in turn the way life proceeds. Similar to a movie script, whatever you write is directed as a movie on the screen. You can make the decision to either write a happy story or a sad story. The pen is in your own hands.

CONSCIOUSNESS

Paradise is not a place, it is a state of consciousness
-Sri Chinmoy

Consciousness is the state of awareness of one's existence, sensations, thoughts, and surroundings. Consciousness can be explained, but it is nearly impossible to comprehend or experience through a mere explanation. Consciousness is difficult to define, because it is not something we can perceive, but rather what does the perceiving. Your eyes allow you to see, and yet you cannot see your own eyes directly. Your mind can possess numerous thoughts, but it is your consciousness that allows you to consider such thoughts and determine the legitimacy of it. Not everyone has the same vision. Some people may suffer from nearsightedness while some may have farsightedness. In extreme cases, some may even suffer from blindness. Likewise, everyone retains different levels of perception and consciousness. It is primarily based on their experiences and understanding of life.

Certain factors, such as ego and false beliefs can obscure your consciousness and act as filters. Ego hides consciousness. If you make a mistake, it doesn't appear to be a mistake from your perspective. On the contrary, if someone else does the same thing, you tend to point it out as a mistake. Consider this statement as food for thought. More often than not, we tend to turn the situation into our favour even if we are wrong. When you were brought into this world, you didn't judge anyone based on beliefs and ego. As you mature, your mind gradually fills with thoughts, beliefs, judgments, and distorted emotions.

When you are conscious, you will not view yourself or others with any judgment or criticism. Consciousness allows us to view different aspects of our self, independently from our mind without judgment. The self is an individual person as the object of your own reflective consciousness. Self-awareness is about being in tune with what you truly think and feel. When you are aware of your thoughts and emotions, you are in control of your life. It is the ability to observe all manners of thoughts, emotions, and beliefs. Every day, a plethora of thoughts run through our mind. The mind works automatically and spontaneously. It only ever needs an improvement program or an occasional update. The primary way to improve the mind is through self-awareness. Once you are entirely aware, then everything proceeds in the right track. It is the conscious awareness you require, to live your life to the fullest.

The more aware you are of these distorting voices in your head, the more conscious you are. The more you judge these voices in your head, the less conscious you are, owing to the fact you return to the egotistic phase once more. Initially, there is a component of consciousness that is perceived as something important. Consequently, this state of consciousness is enveloped with the monkey mind of thoughts, beliefs, and opinions. When you are able to move out and observe the voices in your head, you enter a stage of crystal clear consciousness. A calm mind, devoid of opinions, criticisms, complaints or beliefs, is the ideal way to experience the world consciously, without being clouded by the fog. This indicates the ideal means to perceive and live consciously. In this manner, you will experience the world robustly and beautifully. Society is designed to entrap us in a system of labels and cycles of emotions. Learn to extract your identity from the labels of "winner, loser, success, and failure". In the game of consciousness, the primary mission is to escape your restrictive beliefs, ego, opinions, and labels. It is a necessity to develop control over your attention and sense of self in a different way. The mind is often occupied with the past or with the future always, and it does not think about the present. The state of our mind and our consciousness is like a pendulum, swinging backwards and forwards between the past and the future. Stop dwelling in the past or fantasizing about the future and learn to live in the present moment. Being conscious is to live in the moment now.

According to Advaita, there are four states of consciousness experienced by human beings.

1. The first state is the ***waking state*** (JAGRAT), in which we are aware of our daily world.
2. The second state is the ***dreaming mind*** (SVAPNA).
3. The third state is the state of ***deep sleep*** (SUSUPTI).
4. The fourth state is ***pure consciousness and awareness*** (TURIYA). It is the state of liberation, self-realization, and pure bliss. It is the pure awareness of their own non-dual self, as one with everyone and everything.

Be conscious in every act you do.
Become conscious of Being conscious
-Eckhart Tolle

OBSERVATION

Observe but don't Absorb.

- *Ross Rosenberg*

Observe everything you see, hear, touch, smell, and taste without any judgement. You must observe your thoughts and feelings to understand anything in life. To master the art of observation, you have to give up judging. The art of observation begins with immersing ourselves in the textures and tones of life. Just because you can see does not mean you observe. The difference between seeing and observing is fundamental to many aspects of life. Observation is more than merely looking at something visually; it is the concept of understanding it consciously. Observe every act, every conversation, every reaction, and response. In the case of conflict, separate yourself from ego, observe, and discover the reason for such disputes. A minor change in facial expression formed by those muscles and skin attached to facial bones triggers you to a point where you are forced to retaliate, which in turn forces the opponent to spring into action, leading to the scenario of an unnecessary conflict. Observation helps you to find out the cause for a reaction and hence helps find a solution to the problem.

Paramahamsa Yogananda once said, "By watching the breath, you metaphysically destroy the identification of the soul with the breath and the body. By watching the breath, you separate your ego from it, and know that your body exists only partially by breath". Try to observe the breath flowing up and down along the spine as we inhale and exhale, as if it were the breath of someone else. In this way, you detach yourself from the body. You can change your sense of who you are as not the body, but the ever-observing soul. Witness the whole world around you as a movie. Realize that, all the things you see is nothing but a cosmic motion-picture show. Observe what is happening carefully. Learn to merely observe; avoid getting too caught up with that. Develop a healthy level of silence and stillness. Watch and enjoy the movie but don't become too attached.

Become a *silent observer*, without moving anything in the body. Become completely aware of who and what you truly are, which is pure consciousness. Observe everything as atomic particles and every picture as a light beam and every sound as a vibration.

Listen to every sound and every word you hear around you. Observe how the sound is perceived. Everything is a form of vibration. Sound waves enter your eardrum and in a regulated medium of vibrations, which your brain perceives as that sound you are hearing. When you listen to heavy metal bands, the sound produced by the instruments is transformed from a specific pattern of sound waves in the air to a corresponding pattern of vibrations transmitted through your eardrum, to the small bones located in your middle ear to your cochlea. Then, it is converted neurologically through the auditory nerve to the auditory cortex. This entire network occurring due to vibrations is the experience of the music.

Observe, and in that observation, there is neither the "observer" nor the "observed"-there is only observation taking place. Without the observer, observation cannot take place. Then, you will see in yourself is the whole world.
- J.Krishnamurti

Observe every little detail around you. This book you are currently reading was once part of a living tree, processed into paper, and printed using ink. The printed words depict a means of communication which you can decipher with your eyes and process with your brain, which in turn conveys the message to you, similar to the way I am currently attempting to spread my thoughts to my fellow avid readers. When you observe everything deeply, your experience of life will attain amazing heights.

BELIEFS

If you change the way you look at things,
the things you look at change.
-Wayne Dyer

THE TALE OF THE ELEPHANT AND THE ROPE

Once, a gentleman walking through an elephant camp spotted that the elephants were not kept in cages nor held by the use of chains, but only held by a small piece of rope. Baffled, he asked the trainer how those elephants merely stood still and made no attempts to escape. The trainer replied, "When they were very young and much smaller, we utilized ropes of similar size to tie them, which was enough to hold them. As they matured, they became conditioned to believe they cannot break away from the ropes. They adopted the belief that the rope could still hold them, so they never attempted to break free". Similar to the elephants, many of us go through life clinging onto the belief that we are incapable of doing something, simply because we failed at it once. Every one of us can relate to this story and the feeling of having failed at something or another over the years and never trying again. Over time, we develop the thought that we are incapable of doing such tasks. In turn, we relegate ourselves to this fact and limit ourselves to a very confined world. Occasionally, we try to rewind past experiences and complain about how things didn't turn out as expected. "What is the point in trying it again and wasting my time?" is the common thought that crosses our mind, leading us to settle for less. As soon as a negative thought crosses your mind, learn to expel such thoughts that put you into a state of deep worry and attempt to get rid of your negative beliefs. Beliefs are the source of those thoughts and emotions.

We tend to worry because we believe we are not good enough, smart enough or capable enough to do something leading to a loop of negative thinking. Every instance that negative beliefs cross your mind replace it with positive ones. Keep in mind that patterns of thinking are habitual. Rewrite and reshape your negative beliefs to positive ones and continuously repeat the positive ones to yourself frequently. Respond in a way that is positive by saying, "At least I tried, now I know what doesn't work. Thus the next time I will try harder until I succeed. If your belief system is programmed with an adamant manner of thinking, you are limiting yourself from growth. Your set of beliefs interprets situations automatically and responds without considering any alternatives. Most of your decisions are made in the autopilot system of your unconscious beliefs. This means that almost all your thoughts, emotions, and behaviours are generated automatically. In order to change how you think, feel and act, you need to access these belief systems and tailor them to your requirements.

Prolonged overthinking can magnify minor issues and turn them into the major hindrances, which in turn makes you extremely upset. Your mind goes through a series of associations over the next few minutes or hours together. It creates a chain of narratives linking one thought to another, leading to a loop of emotions.

For example, *when you fail to do something your grandmother requests, she is under the assumption you don't listen to her. Her thoughts may include, "It's like you don't respect me. If you don't respect me, then you don't care about me".*

Every individual has different beliefs and they interpret it through their lens of beliefs. Such beliefs depend on numerous factors such as your mood, emotional state at the time, and the people around you. For example, if you are in a good mood, the joke is perceived as funny, but if you are frustrated and in a bad mood, the joke is deemed annoying. Not everyone has the same set of beliefs. You may have a set of beliefs, but another individual with a different perspective and a different set of beliefs will interpret the same situation differently. A specific situation when someone cracks a joke may offend you. On the contrary, the same situation to your friend may be considered as just comical relief.

Your beliefs and your experiences will help your brain classify how you perceive the events are happening in your life at any given moment. They are the 'Why' behind what you decide to choose. Within mere seconds, your brain processes the input it receives. Everything you see, hear, taste, touch, and smell is processed and analysed in your brain spontaneously before you react or make a decision. Your brain connects the inputs you are experiencing with all of the memories you have ever had or could ever imagine of having, in order to classify your surroundings as good or bad, safe or unsafe. The world as you see it, is a reflection of how you think and perceive. This depends on your beliefs. Your distorted view of the world is more often based on how you perceive reality, rather than how it is. Even though you assume and you are convinced that you are right, just know that the world around you is not always like what it looks like. Your thoughts and your brain form the basis of your reality.

Most of your beliefs happen without your choice or consent and they control your mind. Unless you become aware and begin to take charge of your beliefs, they will continue to have control over your thoughts and emotions. With complete awareness, you can shape your perspective, become the observer of your mind, and avoid getting emotionally caught up in the loop.

You learn who you are by unlearning
who they taught you to be.
- Nikki Rowe

If you can change your beliefs and perception, you can alter the course of your life, leading to a new world of the living. Don't limit yourself to a small world. Stop confining yourself to a life that is restricted, break your mental boundaries and expand your mind. Shatter those negative thoughts and beliefs. Understand your belief system and always maintain a positive outlook. You can do anything, if you believe that you can do it. Having a negative and limiting belief is like wearing a pair of glasses, causing you to always see the world from a perspective with a foggy and obscure vision. Metaphorically, all you need to do is to change the glasses which you wear. It affects every aspect of your life. They influence your emotions, the way you think, the way you respond, the decisions you take, and numerous more aspects of your life. You become a slave to your beliefs, if you fail to understand nor attempt to change them. You can modify any thought pattern, emotional state, and behaviour you desire, if you don't limit yourself with your beliefs.

"Your beliefs become your thoughts, your thoughts become your words, your words become your actions, your actions become your habits, your habits become your values, your values become your destiny."

-Mahatma Gandhi

EMOTIONS

Emotions are involuntary reactions to situations, people, and other factors that affect a person's mental state. Feelings and emotions influence almost everything in our life. Our character and behaviours are directed by emotions. We feel excited when we pass our examination and jump out of joy; we shout and create a ruckus when we become angry, we feel sad at the departure of our loved ones, we tremble when we are afraid. Joy, sorrow, fear, sympathy, empathy, love, and affection are all emotions which influence our life and behaviour. Life would be nothing without emotions and feelings. Emotions play a significant role in how we live our lives and how we behave with others in our day to day lives. They also influence the decisions we make in our life. They have a deeper impact on your behaviour, and understanding them is essential for a happy living. Without a shadow of a doubt, we are ruled by our emotions. We need to take additional responsibility for our emotions. Our life encompasses pain, pleasure, happiness, and sadness. A cumulation of all these makes life interesting. Without emotions, everything would cease to exist and life would be meaningless. The choices we make, the actions we take, and the perceptions we have are all influenced by the emotions we experience at any given moment.

What happens to you when that wave of emotion hits you?

Certain changes occur in your body due to your emotions. We can divide them into external and internal changes.

External changes:

There are many external or observable changes while experiencing an emotion. In particular, your Facial expression changes. It is a fact that the face is the index of the mind. We can easily identify emotions experienced by an individual by looking at his/her face. Your vocal cords move differently and your voice changes according to the type of emotion. At some point, we would have noticed varying pitches when we are excited and also when we are sad. In addition, your body language also changes without your knowledge. You can notice that your hand becomes fidgety, you start biting your nails, your legs move awkwardly, and your body becomes stiff. When you are nervous, you become drenched in your sweat and tears roll down from your eyes.

Internal changes:

Physiology plays a significant role in making internal changes as a response to emotions. The level of your neurotransmitters, such as Dopamine, Serotonin, Acetylcholine, and Norepinephrine determines the internal changes. These internal changes are the result of stimulation of ANS. The ANS has two subdivisions; Sympathetic and Parasympathetic.

Let us consider a leisure Sunday evening when you have nothing to do and decide to relax with your cup of coffee, enjoying every sip of it and listening to your favourite music with an aesthetic view from your balcony while enjoying the cold breeze. When you are CALM and at rest, it is your Parasympathetic System on the field. This determines the way you react when you are in a safe situation without any crisis.

On the next day, it's Monday morning and you suddenly realize that you have a seminar to present and you forgot to prepare for it the previous day as you were just enjoying your prior evening. Now, it's your Sympathetic System on the field. The Sympathetic system prepares your body for facing emergencies and when you are in a crisis, i.e., the fight, fright, and flight response. It stimulates the adrenal glands and makes it to release adrenaline and nor-adrenaline. Adrenaline gets circulated all over the body and stimulates vital organs leading to the internal changes. For example, most of us would have experienced that feeling of insomnia the previous night of our school excursion. Such a feeling is an internal change caused by your excitement. You can experience an increase in your respiratory rate, your heart beats faster than it normally does, your blood pressure rises, and your head feels heavy.

All our emotions have three basic components

The Cognitive Component / The Thinking

It is the voice in your head; what you convey to yourself and interpret about the situation is the cognitive component. A similar situation occurring, which you have already faced before and the way you manage it, is the cognitive component. We label our emotions based on our understanding and interpretation of the situation triggering the emotion. Assume you are waiting for a cab during the night, no one else is nearby and you see a tall person wearing a black jacket sliding his hand into his pocket, which makes you panic. This leads to the emotional experience of fear and the physical reactions associated with the fight-or-flight response. It can be anything; a gun, a phone or whatever. The manner in which you tackle the scenario, usually based on prior experience of a similar instance, maybe from a movie, leads to the emotional experience. The stimulus leads to a physiological response that is then cognitively interpreted and labelled, resulting in an emotion. According to the Cognitive appraisal theory, the sequence of events first involves a stimulus, followed by the thought, which then leads to the simultaneous experience of physiological response and emotion. Your emotional reaction completely depends on how you interpret those physical reactions.

The Physical Component / The Feeling

How you feel inside is the physical component. When questioned, you can easily describe your emotions based on the internal sensations in your body like palpitations, sweating, shortness of breath, fatigue, and a lot more. We may forget the reason for a dispute, but we remember how someone made us feel in that situation. A lot happens inside your body at that moment, physically. Your blood rushes into your veins, you breathe rapidly, your heart beats so fast, you sweat, you clench your teeth, and a surging adrenaline rush. There is a lot to deal with the physiology of your body, when it comes to the component of feeling. Generally, we believe that the physiological changes associated with emotion follow the conscious experience of the individual. Accordingly, we cry because we are sad, we run because we are afraid, and we fight because we are angry. Thus, emotions produce necessary physiological changes and express itself. When a situation takes place and triggers an emotional reaction in you, it makes you feel and react in a certain manner. This feeling component is the heart of your emotion, based on which you respond accordingly.

The Behavioral Component / The Response

The way you respond or react to a certain situation and what you do is the behavioral component. Your behaviour is a direct reflection of your thoughts and it purely depends on the situation. Everyone responds in a unique way to different situations. Certain things can be exciting to you, but not to everyone, thus leading to situations where everyone behaves in their unique way to different situations. Your brain relays the information to your spine, which commands your muscles to respond, thus successfully leading to a particular behaviour. This is a motor and sensory activity. Understanding why you behave in a certain manner is a complicated subject. However, when you analyse it in a deeper aspect, you will discover the exact reason. There are numerous factors which determine your behaviour in different situations and in the presence of different people. Considering a simple example, you tend not to drive your car at the same speed when you drive alone, when you drive with your father, and when you drive with your girlfriend. Reasonably, every behaviour has multiple levels of causality. Your endocrine system plays a huge role in determining your behaviour. What occurs in your head just seconds before you behave in a certain way? Why do you salivate when you see the menu card? After you order your food, you eagerly watch the kitchen door, hoping to see if it was your order. You get disappointed if it is not yours. You become ecstatic when it is your order. What happens during this span? Have you ever thought, why does this happen? It is purely your endocrine system functioning, acting as the director. Your behaviour in turn, can change a situation. When someone triggers your anger, but you fail to respond to it, then the entire scenario shifts.

On the contrary, when you resort to physical violence, it gets reversed. The facial-feedback theory of emotions suggests that facial expressions are connected to experiencing emotions. As mentioned, the face is the index of the mind; our facial expressions play a very vital role in expressing our emotions and for others to understand it. People express their emotions with their facial, vocal, and postural expressions. It helps us to determine how the other person is feeling.

There are different types of emotions that influence our behaviour in the presence of others and how we carry out our living . The six basic emotions experienced are happiness, sadness, disgust, fear, surprise, and anger. These basic emotions have a great impact on human behaviour.

ANGER

For every minute you are angry,
you lose sixty seconds of happiness.
— Ralph Waldo Emerson

Anger is a very powerful emotion characterized by feelings of agitation and frustration towards others. When something triggers your anger, it is that adrenaline rush which flows inside you. It stems from people around you and the individuals that provoke you to elicit such an emotion. When you yell at someone for minor mistakes, your anger can instil fear into someone who makes any mistakes. You tend to become aggressive and behave abruptly, causing you to lose control in such a state of rage. There is a centre in the brain called the Amygdala. If you remove this from your brain, you will not become angry at all, hence ending up turning into a shameless creature. If someone triggers your amygdala, it causes you to burst out in anger in a matter of seconds. Prior experience of abuse or any bitter experiences can make the amygdala of the brain more hyperactive. This makes you angry even for minor issues and will cause you to lose the threshold of your anger. This leads to hastiness and overreaction for simpler situations. For example, you cooked food for your family spending three hours of your leisure Sunday and your husband doesn't appreciate it, rather he complains that the dish is too salty; what happens? He triggers your amygdala and in a few seconds, you become outraged. Adding to this situation, if he includes the same comment in front of his friends or any guests, it is similar to adding fuel to the fire. The environment plays a huge role in your behaviour, so you generally won't express it in front of the guests. However, once they take leave, the husband can rest assured that he receives a sound thrashing later. While anger is often thought of as a negative emotion, it can sometimes be a good thing. It can also help you to take action and find solutions to things that bother you. Anger becomes an issue, when it is excessive and expressed in ways that are dangerous or harmful to others. One should always know to control anger. If not, life will become miserable and you will suffer from negative setbacks. You should choose where, when, and to whom you should display your anger. You cannot choose to hurt your near and dear ones, especially those who care for you. When your wife accidentally spills food on your shirt while serving it on the plate, you may get angry and scold her. However, the same doesn't apply when you are dining at your friend's house or with other co-workers and higher authorities. We tend to display our anger towards people who are at a level that doesn't retaliate, people who are close to our heart, and people who genuinely care about us. Anger can have both mental and physical consequences. You should always keep track of your anger. Uncontrolled anger can make your life difficult and can be detrimental towards your life and the people around you.

We all possess a threshold for anger. When someone triggers your anger, first analyse the situation and find out the reason for such a reaction. If it is someone else's mistake, try to reason with them and arrive at an understanding. Be in the present, try to be calm, and accept that nothing can be done about a situation that has passed and focus on the future course of action. It is natural to be angry at someone and want to seek some form of retribution. However, you will only attract negative things to your life in such cases. Revenge isn't always the best option. Seeking actual revenge against someone shifts the focus of the mind in the wrong direction. Ask yourself a series of questions regarding the situation; What made you so angry? What could you learn from this situation? Where was the mistake? Why did you feel that way? How to avoid it in the future when a similar situation arises? What would be a better approach rather than getting on your nerves?

Before you pull the trigger, give it some time and analyse. You may say hurtful things in the heat of the moment, and it can burn you for a lifetime. Avoid losing your cool and learn to direct your attention to something else immediately. Sit and think about it. Analyse your emotions and adjust your response accordingly. You gain nothing by anger. You're a human being and there is nothing wrong in being angry. However, when you are always angry and it gets out of control, it becomes a problem. Everyone has their own set of problems and frustrations, which affects their behaviour and thoughts.

It can take advantage of you and will eventually take over your personality and turn you into someone else, as if you were hypnotized by it temporarily. Later on, you will be baffled if you really said such things. Go ahead and vent out your frustrations. However, avoid overreacting to it, but react responsibly when it hits you hard. Try to look at it from another perspective. Watch yourself being drawn into it and then learn to disregard it. Also, watching it from a third person vision helps immensely. We tend to label it as just anger, but there is far more behind that. It can arise from self-judgment, self-hate, guilt, shame, past experiences, beliefs, and numerous more reasons behind your anger. The following few methods will teach you to manage your anger.

ACCEPT

Acceptance is the key to eliminate anger. Regardless of the situation, you have to learn to accept it. You expect something to happen in a certain way, but it doesn't turn out as expected.

Thus, it leads to your amygdala being triggered and in turn, a series of events takes place in your head. You have to accept and realise the fact that not everything happens in a programmed way and anything can happen out of the blue. It is as if we don't read the pages of the terms and conditions when we download something and we proceed just to click ACCEPT to the terms and conditions checkbox. If your friend broke your favourite pair of glasses, he/she would not have done it on purpose. Rather, it would have slipped from their hand and broke. You have to accept the fact that the glass once broken cannot return to its original state. Thus, it would be foolish to get upset over something that can be fixed in exchange for a valuable friendship. Some people get angry and frustrated because of their appearance. It doesn't matter if you are dark, short or fat. Firstly, it is because of your genes and you have to accept that simple fact. Secondly, think about improving your appearance in different possible ways. Simply stated, accept the unchangeable and change the changeable.

FORGIVE

Holding on to anger is like holding a knife tightly, it will only hurt you in the long run. Forgive, but don't forget the valuable lessons that the situation taught you and how it made you feel at that instance. Let go of that negative energy and learn to forgive. Your mind will feel much more at ease.

AVOID HASTY ACTIONS

Quick decisions made impulsively always end in regret. You need to give it time. Before making a decision when you are angry, halt for a moment and think. Choices made in anger cannot be undone. Words spoken in anger can't be taken back. Time will heal all wounds and everything will be fine in a certain frame of time. Don't fire something off like a text message or make a call when you're at the peak of anger. Wait and think, give it some time and avoid doing anything at the spur of that moment without thinking of the consequences.

MAINTAIN ANGER CHART

Track your anger every day. Make a chart and mark what triggers you to lose control at that moment. When you do this on a regular basis, you will definitely maintain a level of control over it. However, it is difficult to give up your anger issues in an instant. It is a challenging task that requires immense self-control and tolerance. It only comes with practice. With frequent practice, you can overcome the anger that destroys your peace of mind. Furthermore, the people around you can also live a peaceful and happy life.

DISTRACT YOURSELF

Shift away your focus from the problem, making you angry. There are a lot of ways to distract yourself from such an issue. Go for a jog or watch something funny that can make you forget everything. Laughter is nature's tool for healing. Sit back and relax for a while. After a turbulent situation, it's good just to relax. It feels good to disconnect and laugh a bit. Don't take life so seriously. Live every moment and realise that it could all be gone tomorrow.

IGNORANCE IS BLISS

Learning to ignore things is one of the most significant paths of inner peace. Ignorance is bliss, only when you know what to ignore. It is okay to ignore a phone call or a text from a person if it triggers your anger or disturbs your peace of mind. Ignore it just like that. It is futile to spend your valuable energy on people or situations which exhausts you.

DON'T CHOOSE THE WRONG PATH

Don't drink or do drugs or do anything else that will intensify your current feelings. When you are already angry and you choose to drink, you enter a foggy state of mind to make wrong decisions which will affect you. It is always better to make decisions when you are fully conscious than under the influence of something external, which can lead you in a wrong path.

FIND YOUR SOLUTION

Methods of managing anger are not the same for everyone. Similar to how every individual has a different fingerprint, everyone will have different ways of coping with anger. Whatever methods you tried to manage your anger and other emotions during the earlier stages of your life is not guaranteed to work as you become older. When you are angry at someone at the age of 16, you may resort to physical violence. However, the same can't be said when you are at an age of 60, which may ironically lead you to hurt yourself. The mind prefers to maintain consistency with past actions, even if it doesn't work anymore. You need to find ideal solutions which will work at this stage of your life. Break down your problem of anger into smaller steps and try to find appropriate solutions.

SEE FROM THE OPPONENT'S SPECS

Place yourself in the shoes of your adversary. Try to think about how they may feel, what your anger does to them, and how it can adversely affect them. Analyse the reason for their passive-aggressiveness that made you angry. For example, assume your employee arrives late at the office and you yell at him. What you may not know is that he would have had to deal with a list of problems on his way to the office. It may be an issue with the vehicle, an accident, personal health issues, and other such factors. Everything doesn't proceed perfectly as you imagine it should every day. Everyone has their own set of problems and anything can happen to anyone. Imagine yourself in the same situation, as a victim at the receiving end of someone else's frustration. Now, do you want to make someone feel that bad because of your state of anger? Try to look at it from their perspective. Analyse the situation and change your thinking, so that you can look at things differently and behave aptly. In short, avoid being angry all the time.

KARMA

When a bird is alive, it eats Ants.
When the bird is dead, Ants eat the bird.
Time & Circumstances can change at any time.
Don't devalue or hurt anyone in life.
You may be powerful today.
But remember, Time is more powerful than you.
SO BE GOOD AND DO GOOD.
Don't take revenge, let karma do all the work"
-BUDDHA

When something triggers your anger and affects you deeply, but you end up powerless to be able to do anything about it, just allow Karma to play its role. The word Karma itself can help mitigate your anger and can also create fear when you do something wrong. Karma will act on its own, in accordance with its own Law. Before you decide to take revenge, always remember what goes around, comes around.

It is ill-advised to hurt an individual when you are angry physically. Eventually, everyone will get what they deserve. If someone intentionally harmed you, it will come back to them. It might take a while for that to occur, but it will happen. You should not harm someone just because they chose to indulge in malicious means. It is all about the cycle of cause and effect. According to the theory of Karma, what happens to a person, happens because they triggered it with their actions.

FEAR

Fear kills more dreams than failure ever will.
Living in fear is not living at all
- Christopher

Fear is an emotional response to an immediate threat.

It is a natural response that plays an essential role in survival. When you are faced with a dangerous scenario, your body either runs from the danger or allows you to stand your ground. You sweat profusely, your heart beats faster, and you breathe rapidly when you are experiencing fear. Almost anything can incite fear. Fear of losing something you have now, fear of dying, fear of living, fear of failure, and the list goes on. When you are the only person walking on the street and a group of stray dogs start barking at you, you feel fear. Even our thoughts about potential dangers can cause fear. Analysing fear a bit deeper, when your mind imagines a scenario, your body responds to it. The fear created is clearly a response from your thoughts and beliefs. We usually describe it in one word, but it is a combination of several thoughts and beliefs.

When we are repeatedly exposed to a certain type of fear, the power of that emotion decreases. It is similar to resistance to a drug when we utilise it quite often. This is called exposure therapy. When you are gradually exposed to the things that frighten you in a controlled and safe manner, the feeling of fear decreases with time. We fear the first time we drive a car on the road. However, with continuous exposure practise, we can overcome it. We should expose ourselves to our deepest fears to make it through. Imaginary scenarios and negative thoughts are the primary reasons for fear. Fear exists within your head and your brain cannot tell the difference between a real scenario and one we imagine. Fear is an essential emotion, according to me. Without fear, we will be stuck in many dangerous situations. However, an issue is that your mind can generate too many fearful scenarios and negative thoughts unnecessarily. The root cause of all fear is your thoughts. When you eliminate the process of witnessing or hearing something terrifying, you will learn not to be afraid. Nevertheless, fear is essential for survival in certain situations. If you do not have a fear of examination, you will not study and ultimately end up failing.

Fear is always due to external factors; it does not exist by itself. Your thoughts of what occurred in the past and what will happen in the future, creates more of your fear than what is currently happening in the present. It is your thoughts that bring and escorts fear. We lose most of our happy and peaceful moments by the mere thought of uncertainty.

In some instances, some individuals even fear the thought of being happy, which is termed as Cherophobia. It is the fear of happiness, owing to certain individuals who believe that any time they feel too happy, something bad will eventually happen.

Our childhood plays a major impact on our current fears. A fearful event which happened when you were a child, can leave you scarred throughout your life. That particular fearful response when you were young, might still reside within you. It should be accepted, reprogrammed, and updated. Being alone is a fear of loneliness. This can cause your mind to imagine a future where you are left alone, without someone to love or care about you. Now, fear gives rise to sadness and leads to depression. A baby, when left alone, cries because of the fear of being alone. Similarly, the same thought of isolation resides until you become brave and learn to survive in a situation where you have to be alone and independent. The thought of someone not being beside us is perfectly natural, which is an instinctual fear that a vast majority of us already experienced prior to learning how to think and speak. These strong emotions and associations to being alone can be stored and repressed in your memory. You are programmed to be in fear when you are alone or even by the thought of being alone, which your mind automatically connects to that specific memory and feeling of fear. When someone you love does not pick up the call or doesn't respond to your texts for a long time, you immediately feel that they don't care about you anymore. However, there may exist many reasons for not responding; they might be busy with important work, maybe asleep or may not even have put their phone with them. Your mind does not easily accept this situation. Instinctively, this makes you think there is no one to turn to, leading to a feeling of abandonment. A long movie plays out in your mind. You start to form a perception in your mind about how the people around you should be. In other words, you begin to have expectations. When the unexpected occurs, it leads to disappointment, which ultimately leads to fear and is converted to anger with time. Infusing unnecessary fear by unnecessary thinking is called *OVERTHINKING*. It kills your happiness by creating or thinking about problems that never exist.

Being aware of the root of your fear and knowing how they occur is the key to eliminate fear. You just have to change the way you think about it and alter your perception.

HAPPINESS

"Happiness can be found even in the darkest of times, if only one remembers to turn on the light."

– Dumbledore

Happiness is a pleasant emotional state and is one of the basic human emotions that is characterised by feelings of joy, peace, and satisfaction. Happiness is influenced by numerous factors such as the people around you, your mindset, and so on. It is an individual's perception; you may be happy with one thing but not necessarily happy with something different. It becomes difficult for you to find happiness internally if your attention is focused on external factors. Those feelings will have to be inspired and discovered within yourself. The happiness you derive when you consume your favourite food, watch a movie, when someone compliments you or when you receive positive feedback on your social media post is all external. Happiness originates from within. If you cannot find true happiness inside yourself, you cannot hope to find it in the outside world. Happiness is something you discover and it emerges from the way you think. It is not relevant to what you possess, who you are, where you live, or what you do for a living, that makes you happy; it is based on how you think. A beggar can be the happiest man and a multimillionaire can remain miserable. It depends on the way you think, perceive, and interpret everything. When your happiness depends on the outside world, it is of no guarantee that it will be permanent. Change your beliefs, stop judging, and cleanse your negative emotions. These simple tips will enable you to live as a completely changed individual.

Tame your inner self

Commandeer control over the voice in your head that whispers, "Someone is watching and will make fun of you, so you should not do that". Do whatever makes you happy. Tame your thoughts. There is no need to notice everything and not everything needs your reaction. It is entirely okay to let go in certain situations. In such cases, try to enter a thoughtless state. Let things happen as they should happen. Just go with the flow. Life becomes a joyful journey if you learn to look at it from a different perspective. Consider everything as a valuable lesson and let it happen. Don't worry about everything. Ignore what makes you sad. Your level of happiness should not be determined by something external. Do whatever feels right and makes you happy.

You are responsible for your own happiness.

Seven simple steps for Happiness

Think less, Feel More,

Frown Less, Smile More,

Talk Less, Listen More,

Judge Less, Accept More,

Watch Less, Do More,

Complain Less, Appreciate More,

Fear Less, Love More.

SADNESS

Sadness is a transient emotional state characterised by feelings of disappointment, hopelessness, grief, and disinterest. From time to time, everyone will experience sadness. There is nothing wrong in being sad, but staying in such a state for a prolonged duration of time can be dangerous and can lead to depression. Don't let it take over you. Try to find out the reason for your sadness. Find the root cause and attempt to pinpoint a solution. Turn your negative emotion to a positive one. When you are disappointed with something, don't dwell on it. Instead, stop being sad and formulate methods to cope with it and move on.

DISGUST

Disgust is an emotional response to rejection. This depends on your beliefs and past experiences. You feel disgusted by something you perceive with your physical senses such as sight, smell, touch, sound and taste, actions or behaviour of people, and even by ideas. This sense of disgust can originate from several factors. It can be summarised as a reaction when you don't like something. Disgust helps you to change something you detest certain things. Only when you know what you dislike, can you do more of what you want. Only when you discover doing something repulsive, will you learn to change that behaviour.

SURPRISE

Life is full of surprises, but the biggest one of all is learning what it takes to handle them.

-Deborah Wiles

When a sudden and unexpected incident occurs, you are surprised. This can be positive or even negative, depending on the situation. Surprise is another type of emotion that can trigger the fight or flight response. When startled, people may experience a burst of adrenaline. A positive surprise automatically leads to happiness and a negative surprise leads to sadness. This kind of emotion is mostly based on external factors. For example, you arrive home from work and you find all your friends have gathered to celebrate your birthday; it denotes a surprise. It is sudden and unexpected and you are happy to see them after a long time. There is a sudden spark of happiness inside you. It is kind of exciting. It just happens naturally. Sometimes, you may receive a negative surprise during the sudden demise of someone dear to you. This can be an agonising situation, but requires acceptance to move on. Learn to accept and acknowledge the fact that surprises and unexpected events are part and parcel of your life.

Emotional Awareness

When you are entirely aware of your emotions, you are in complete control. Emotional awareness is the first step towards building emotional intelligence. Emotional awareness simply means recognising, respecting, and accepting your feelings as they happen. Analyse and track your emotions every single day.

Ask yourself,

1. How do you feel?
2. What made you feel that way?
3. What should you do to be happy and at peace?

Ask these questions throughout the day in different situations. Track your emotions throughout the day and if you happen to encounter any negative emotions, act hastily and try to find a quick solution to alter your current predicament as soon as possible. When you are aware of your emotions, you are in complete control of your life.

Never let your emotions overpower your intelligence.
Learn to master your emotions.

WORRY

Worrying is using your imagination to create something you don't want

-Abraham Hicks

It is natural to worry and stress about a situation. We worry about our past, present, and future in general. Worrying can become a habit that becomes ingrained in mind and can prevent you from truly living your life. Like any other habit, it is possible to quit worrying and start living your life to the fullest by remembering a few key principles in your mind to break the habit. It is easy to advise someone to stop worrying. In reality, it is difficult to implement. Worrying releases stress hormones such as adrenaline and cortisol, which negatively impacts us mentally and physically. You will get more of what you desire if you maintain focus on your target. Realise that our subconscious minds control our lives. Progressive thoughts in your mind will place you in the right track. If you focus on only problems, you'll encounter more problems. If you focus on something positive, eventually you'll start seeing positive things, steering your life in that direction. It is hard to shift your focus overnight, but it is something that you can do gradually over time. This doesn't mean you have to ignore your problems. You have to acknowledge them, but also simultaneously focus on the solutions. The situation only aggravates if you constantly worry about it rather than finding a solution. When you frequently worry about something, the outcome doesn't change unless you take the right step forward to change it. For example, when you are carrying a hefty bag, you choose to drop off all the unnecessary items and take only the essentials with you.

Similarly, you can't hope to shoulder all your burdens throughout the day. You can soar high only if you drop them off. When you constantly load your mind with worries, you will eventually end up depressed. Certain factors can't be changed and stressing on them is of no use. Worrying why a stone is hard is not going to melt it away.

Ask yourself, "Why am I so worried?" The right course of action would be to find a solution. More often than not, we worry about the fear of failure that we provide space for such thoughts in our mind, which is far worse than actual failure itself. Always be optimistic and give no room for negative thinking. Realise and remember that you managed to pull through in the past, and you'll pull through again. You did it once before and you can do it again. Worrying never improves the situation. Often, we worry about what other people would think of us in the event of doing particular actions. There will always be people to judge you and speak ill of you behind your back. In such cases, the ideal course of action is to not worry about their opinions. Don't let someone's opinion of you become your reality. You are here to live your life. Thus, don't worry about what others might think and live your life in your unique way.

SCHEDULE TIME TO WORRY

Schedule 20 minutes a day just to vent out your worries. This is to acknowledge the problems and to specifically work through the things that we may be worried about. When you are in such a situation, ask yourself if it is worth worrying and spending your precious time on. Grade it on a scale of 1 to 10. Make a strategic plan, take action, and attempt to solve the problem. Don't waste your time constantly pondering upon the problem. The situation doesn't improve if we sit idly and expect our problems to go away.

EGO

The ego is nothing other than the focus of conscious attention.

-Alan Watts

The word ego means "I" in Latin. It is simply considering yourself first and being selfish. A motive is egoistic when it is focused on what "I" want and to act on one's self-interest. Ego is your conscious mind; the part of your identity that you consider your "self". An egoistic individual will consciously and continuously think about only what they want, what they are doing, who they are, what other people think about them, and how things are going for them. They are highly self-absorbed, self-centred and their reactions concern only themselves. They disagree with other people, even on minor things and are under the assumption that only they can travel on the righteous path and will even go so far as to prove their point. Our perception of the world is always a blend of objective reality and our interpretation of reality. No one can see the world from any perspective other than their own. It feels as if only we are capable of seeing things clearly and are correct.

Self-image develops when we are praised or criticized for our actions. When you secure top grades, you are praised. On the contrary, when you fail, you get teased and end up forming a negative self-image. Teasing and criticizing may cause the individual to feel worthless. To mask the pain, they may try to cover it up with a false image of confidence, whilst struggling with their own feelings of insecurity and worthlessness. In turn, they try to keep it bottled up inside, which leads to depression. Ego hijacks any form of analysis and turns it into a self-criticism/blame process. When the ego controls the self-reflection process, you stand no chance of identifying the root cause of your emotion. Ego is usually associated with arrogance and is a term used to describe someone who thinks they are better than others. Every individual's ego is different and is built upon different beliefs and past experiences acquired over their course of life. Ego based beliefs of being right and knowing better than someone else, triggers emotions. A person can be immensely successful and confident in what they do, without allowing it to get into their heads. It is difficult to highlight the differences between ego and the inner true character. In a way, ego masks one's true inner self.

We spend years building our ego self-images, living inside of them, and reinforcing them. Extracting our genuine self out of this matrix of false beliefs will require extensive time and effort. Even when we recognize that our egocentric perspective and beliefs may contaminate our views, we still interpret that we are on the right path. As an individual, one tends to possess a narrow, one-sided view. Ego can be compared to a person in a dark room with a torch; anything beyond the reach of the torch beam isn't visible. It is your EGO and unconscious BELIEFS that operates out of impulse automatically, causing all the chaos in your life. Being aware of your thought process is the antidote to your ego. It allows you to silence your own mind, remain calm, and think clearly. Detach yourself from individual thoughts and let go of the beliefs, separating yourself from the false identity of your ego.

PART TWO

SETUP AND PROGRAMMING

DECLUTTER

If you want to fly, you have to give up the things that weigh you down
- Toni Morrison

Detaching yourself from whatever is meaningless and weighs you down is essential for a peaceful mind. Discard all unnecessary and futile thoughts running through your mind, similar to how you discard useless junk every day. You cannot hope to think clearly with a multitude of thoughts running through your mind. For example, your phone won't operate efficiently if you keep running all the unwanted applications in the background. To solve this, you clear the background apps and optimize it.

Similarly, clear off all unnecessary thoughts from your mind. You have to flush away thoughts of the past holding you back. When your mind is cluttered with numerous thoughts, it can't think nor function properly. It creates mental confusion and distraction, which prevents you from making clear decisions. Clearing the clutter out of your mind will help you to focus on the right track and will aid you to be productive. Decluttering is an art of retaining what you want and discarding what you don't need.

SET UP YOUR PLACE RIGHT

The safest and easiest way that can help you to think clearly is to start by decluttering your workspace and setting up a proper ambience. Unnecessary belongings occupying your room will have an adverse impact on your ability to think and make decisions. Don't attempt to get rid of everything. Instead, try to retain only the essential items. Keep your space simple and organize it properly with limited possessions. Your ambience has a great impact on your state of mind. In order to lift your spirits, try lighting up a scented candle and playing Beethoven's symphony or Mozart in the background. Changing the little things around you, will have a huge impact on the way you think and your mindset. Start by getting rid of all of the meaningless things around you that serve no purpose.

SCRIBE

Now that your workplace is devoid of clutter, focus on clearing your mind. Pen down all your thoughts on paper. The best way to declutter your mind is to consolidate all those thoughts running through your mind and convert them in writing. This will aid you in making organized decisions and also helps you to declutter your mind instantly. After writing down all the things running through your head, proceed to plan and organize. This guides you to differentiate between tasks that require your time and energy and mere useless junk accumulating your mind. Journaling is a therapy. It helps you organize your thoughts and understand your emotions. Journaling is a great way to relax your mind by analyzing and organizing your thoughts.

SET AND COMPLETE PRIORITIES

Make a to-do list of all the important tasks you need to complete, and start prioritizing them. The list may be long but don't worry. Once you dump your to-do list by writing down your tasks, begin to categorize them according to priority. Find that everything that you are jotting down feels important. You can further identify items that are *urgent*—meaning if you fail to complete them by today, it will have serious negative consequences. Prioritizing will help you become clear and organized. In keeping track of your to-do list, the first step is to figure out the tasks that matter the most to you. Prepare a list of your top priorities and make sure that your actions and the decisions you make takes one step closer to your goal. Create an action plan to achieve those goals and assign time to focus on each individual item on that list. Postponing your work and accumulating a lot of pending tasks is the sole cause for mental clutter. Even if it is a minor task, plan and complete it as soon as possible. Accumulating tasks will automatically lead to stress, which eventually accumulates into a heap of tasks when left undone. Carefully evaluate the pros and cons and avoid looking back once you've made up your mind to complete a task. When you complete your tasks one by one and strike them off your to-do list, you will attain a sense of satisfaction from accomplishing a potentially difficult task from your to-do list. Reward yourself for completing a task and proceed to shorten your to-do list by completing further tasks.

SHARE YOUR THOUGHTS

Sharing your thoughts with someone you can trust and genuinely cares for you, will help you look at things from a different perspective. This can help you think in a clear manner and make better decisions. Sometimes, venting out and sharing your problems with someone can be of immense help and will make you feel light. Talking to your loved ones about how you feel is a great way to release dumped emotions and will help to clear your mind.

LIMIT YOUR SOCIAL MEDIA INTAKE

The primary source of a vast majority of mental clutter nowadays is due to social media. When you keep track of your mind, you would have noticed your mind getting flooded with thoughts and feelings from posts and stories of other people on social media. Just the mere thought of seeing a picture, of someone doing something, will make you jealous for not being able to participate in such a similar situation. At the same time, you are stuck at home, relegated to just looking at such pictures and responding to it. What someone else does is none of your business. It is healthier to mind our own business and be at peace. Concentrate on improving yourself daily. Social media is very addictive and consumes your precious time. Avoid using it for more than 30 minutes a day. You can start by setting a limit on the amount of time you spend on social media and also learning to be selective about your media consumption by following positive subjects and avoiding negative content.

SLEEP

When your brain is cluttered with a plethora of thoughts and continuously causes you to focus on your problems, try to get some rest. Sound sleep can solve almost all your problems. It calms you down, helps you with your mental state, helps you make better decisions, and solves problems. It is not about ignoring the problem, but it is about handling your stress. When your problem bothers you to an extent that you are unable to catch some sleep, just take a deep breath and remember that everything in life is temporary, including the thoughts running through your mind. Be optimistic and believe that you can solve it. Try listening to melodies such as Weightless by Marconi union or any relaxing music in the background, which will definitely ease your mind. Your brain will get exhausted if you keep thinking all the time. Forget everything and try to get ample rest—sleep deep you wonderful soul.

MEDITATE

Meditation is a simple process to declutter your mind and it brings clarity of thought. When you meditate, all your confusion disappears and it allows you to make clear decisions and helps in focusing on what is important. Take some time to meditate daily and make it a routine.

BREATHE

Take a deep breath, inhale slowly, and exhale slowly. Do this consciously. Deep breathing is a simple yet effective technique to clear your mind. Observe your breath closely. When you are angry or afraid of something, your breath is more rapid and short. However, when you are comfortably sleeping, your breath is slower and longer. Imagine yourself inhaling positivity and exhaling negativity. While breathing in, sink this thought of "I AM NOT THE BODY", and while breathing out "I AM NOT THE MIND". This instantly elevates your mood. It stimulates the parasympathetic nervous system which helps your body to relax by decreasing the heart rate and blood pressure. Learn to let go of your thoughts. It is essential to let go of all the negative thoughts and emotions that make you feel low. Eliminating those thoughts helps to free up mental space. Maintain a track of your thoughts and be conscious of what you are always thinking.

FREE YOUR BODY

Declutter your body from all the stress you have accumulated. Practice freeing your body. Relax every muscle. Remove any form of stress from your body and just let go. When you are alone in your place of zen, just let yourself loose. Relax by playing some calm music and try not to let anything demoralize you. There is no harm in grooving to the rhythm of the music. Dance like nobody's watching. This can help you overcome inhibitions and to find your true self.

THROW AWAY YOUR WORRIES

Worrying is natural. However, when your worries consume your mind and keep you worried all day, it becomes a problem. Worrying is bound to not change anything. Instead of worrying, attempt to find a solution to the problem. Allowing the same series of actions to run through your mind won't give you peace of mind. Schedule a time for worrying. At the most, 30 minutes at the end of a long day. Don't hold back any emotions and just let it run its course. Discard them away from your mind. By confining your worries to a scheduled time, you don't allow them to take over your mind and life.

TAKE A BREAK

Go for a walk, listen to music, or do something that makes you blissful. Everyone needs their personal space to unwind, which cannot be achieved if the mind is cluttered with redundant thoughts. Take a break to your thinking process and avoid any form of worthless thoughts. We need this special time and space in our lives in order to remember who we really are. It is our personal allocated time to calm the spirit and soothe the soul. Simply being still and quiet for a period of time brings much peace. Sit back, relax, and appreciate your life, recognize how far you have come. Free up your mental space and just go with the flow. Your brain needs to rest and recharge to perform smoothly.

JOURNALING

Journaling is a potent and powerful habit. It helps us to improve in every aspect of our life. Most of us have the habit of checking our phone or social media immediately when we wake up. What we do in the morning influences our entire day. Instead of checking your phone, practice writing your journal. Spend just 10 minutes to plan your day or maybe pen down your thoughts at the moment. Journaling helps you to make an in-depth analysis and evaluation of your experiences. This increases your self-awareness and helps in all aspects of your life. Journaling is a beautiful and powerful facilitator of self-discovery. There are numerous benefits to keeping a journal.

ORGANISE YOUR THOUGHTS

Keeping a journal can help you to organize your thoughts. Jot down your daily events, thoughts, experiences, and opinions. When you begin writing, you eventually acknowledge the important aspects of your life and the requisites to improving it. Writing creates spatial regions between important and non-important pieces of information, helping us to focus on important stuff. It helps you to think, analyse, perceive and interpret differently and positively.

STRESS BUSTER

Writing down your feelings can be of immense help to relieve stress. Most of us bottle up our emotions and feelings, which may even lead to depression. This can even affect our life to a great extent, owing to the sequence of repetitive thoughts. Whatever feelings you have deep down inside you, write it down in your journal. Writing is a therapy which clears your head. This can help relieve stress in the long run.

MANIFEST YOUR GOALS

Journaling accelerates your ability to manifest your goals. As you make a note of your goals daily and read them, they will enter your subconscious mind. Eventually, your dreams will manifest and become a physical reality. A journal is an excellent place to write your goals and ambitions. Writing them down can help you track and monitor your progress towards your goal. It allows you to be productive and focus on the ideal path.

CLARITY OF THOUGHT

Writing down your thoughts on a paper can provide crystal-clear clarity of your thoughts and helps you in making better decisions. Writing allows your subconscious mind to function without problems in unique ways.

TRACK YOUR DAY

When you wake up in the morning instead of checking your phone, open up your journal and spend 10 minutes planning your day. Write it down. This helps you to be on track and you won't feel lost. It gets registered in your subconscious mind and constantly reminds you to complete your task. Provide critical feedback on how you performed, how you felt, and what you could have done better at the end of the day. This can help you keep track of your progress. You can also employ a mood tracker to check how you felt throughout the day. Make yourself accountable for what you finished on that day and what needs to be done tomorrow. At the end of the day, your journal should show you the list of your progress and mistakes.

Appreciate yourself for your progress and correct those mistakes. It helps you to self-reflect on what you did today and what you can do to improve yourself. This practice will definitely increase your productivity to a much greater extent.

AS A DIARY

Describe your daily experience. Write about the tasks you did today, what you thought about, or what happened around you today. Journaling records your life history. We forget most of the events of our life. We are bad at retaining information. Keeping a journal can give you a chance to create and consider the narrative element of your life, with all of the choices you have made and the memories you wish to cherish.

WRITING THERAPY

Journaling can help you experience, understand, and handle your emotions. For hours, days, and even years together, specific thoughts and emotions may linger. Journaling can help you find a solution to break away from the issues that bother you. It *helps you in critical self-analysis. It* will make you realize the set of circumstances that keeps holding you back and adequate steps that could be taken to resolve them. It helps you to identify and accept your emotions. Writing your thoughts, feelings, and actions in a journal will allow you to look deep into your soul. In addition, it helps to discover your authentic identity. It can help you establish important connections between thoughts, feelings, and your behaviour. Effective journaling is the best form of therapy.

AFFIRMATION JOURNALING

Affirmations are positive statements, that can help you overcome your negative thoughts. When you repeat them often and believe in them, you can start to see positive changes. It may seem, like affirmations are unrealistic "wishful thinking", but in hindsight, they are similar to programming your subconscious mind. You may either write it down or allow it to persist in your mind. An affirmation requires you to focus on something specific; the more specific the better. Write and orate your affirmations, as if it is a current ongoing process. Believe in it strongly and feel like you already have achieved it. Affirmations can rewire your brain. They can help us to stay focused and motivated.

Start your day by writing,

"Today is going to be the best day of my *life*",
and believe it without any doubt.

This is equivalent to programming your entire day when you initiate. Spend the first few minutes of your day by writing affirmations and you can see it manifest intensely, similar to a magic wish book. Write down whatever changes you want to make in your life or however you want your life to be. When you pen down your affirmations on the paper, it gets registered deeply in your subconscious mind.

Try writing:

I am happy, healthy, and in love with my life.
I am a unique being with amazing abilities.
I attract positive things and people in my life.
I choose to do great things today.
Today I will enjoy every moment to the fullest.
Today I will be kinder, smarter and wiser.
I am in charge of my life.
I am aligned with my higher self.
I manifest abundance easily.
I am ready to start the day.

GRATITUDE JOURNALING

Make a note of all that you are thankful for. Think of it as a thank you letter to the universe. When you start writing about the things you're grateful for, it can make you more optimistic, as you make the conscious decision to see more of the positivity in your life. You can write about whatever makes you happy; it may be your family, friends, your pet, your favourite food or anything 4you enjoy. Describe the scenario and mention how happy you are and thank the universe for making it happen. Gratitude journaling can bring about immense positive changes on the way you perceive the world around you.

Try to pen down all that you are grateful for.

I am grateful that I woke up today.
I am grateful that I am alive and awesome.
I am grateful that I can breathe, see, hear, talk, walk, eat, and do everything I want.
I am grateful for this beautiful, healthy body I have
I am grateful for the life I have.
I am grateful for all the people that I have in my life.
I am grateful for all the opportunities I have.
I am grateful for the work I do now.
I am grateful for everything that I have.
I am grateful for every second of my life.

Thank you, universe, for this new day

When you are puzzled regarding the content you wish to write about, record your current state of thoughts on paper, without a moment's hesitation. Take a brief moment to remain still, calm, focused, and enter a state of reminiscence. Analyse your thoughts and feelings through your writing. The concept of writing a journal is to empty your mind off your thoughts.

YOUR TWENTY-FOUR HOURS

This moment, this very moment you are living is more important than your past or the future. Don't dwell in the past, for it is of no use. What you have now is the present moment. If you make appropriate and optimum use of the present moment, then you will definitely have a better future.

To some people, it is merely one day. However, it consists of 24 hours or 1440 minutes. One should realize the magnitude of tasks that could be accomplished in these 24 hours. When you manage this 24-hour time frame effectively, you can achieve a lot of things. Time management is the key to success. It allows you to take control of your life. When you don't have control of your time, you will end up with immense stress and confusion. Without proper time management, it feels as if we are always engaged aimlessly and don't possess adequate time to relax. Once you learn how to manage your time, everything changes for the better and your life feels back on track and organized.

Ask yourself this question every day, 'If today was the last day of my life, would I do what I am about to do today?'

All of us have the same 24 hours a day; nothing more, nothing less. It is how we manage and utilize the time that makes the difference in our life. Every moment is precious. Every second is of infinite value. If you have ever had someone close to you pass away, you would already know that every moment is precious. Life is short. Don't be lazy and waste your time. It is better to make the utmost use of the time we have, instead of regretting afterwards because time once gone never comes back. There is so much that we need to accomplish and achieve in our lives. When you are old and reflect upon your past, you will definitely regret all the time you wasted idly on your bed watching that dumb box or scrolling your social media feed. Once time passes, it is lost forever. Don't spend time doing things that don't add any form of value to your life. Invest your time on things that will help you live the life of your dreams. Don't be wasting away your time into nothingness. Make use of your time and be productive. Live a life you will remember and be proud of. Make memories, but don't waste time doing anything. The time you enjoy is not time wasted.

More often than not, we feel that we don't have enough time every day. We all wish we had more time in a day. When the day is over and we look back at what we accomplished, we often ponder upon all of those hours which passed us by. Instead of swiping your phone screen continuously or binge-watching a series, get out there and spend your time with the people you love. Learn to step outside of your comfort zone. It doesn't require much of your effort. All it takes is the willingness to change. Even if you don't spend your time with others, avoid wasting it. Time can never be re-created; thus, you have to use it wisely. Squeeze every last second out of the day and make it worthwhile.

When the sun shines and your alarm beeps in the morning, don't immediately snooze it. Wake up, rise and shine, for it is a brand new day filled with pleasant activities. Plan your day accordingly and be productive. Pursue your passions. Do something great that adds value to your life. Become a better human each day. Enjoy every second of your life.

SET YOUR GOALS

Decide exactly what you want, why you want it, and by when you want it. Write it down to the very last detail. You might think to yourself that, you already know what you want, and you maintain mental notes of it in your mind. However, writing down your tasks on a paper is remarkably different, then merely setting them in your head. Be clear on what you plan on doing all day and pen it down. This will help you to stay on track. Once you understand why you want something deep down inside, then you'll take adequate measures to get you there. Question yourself deeper and try to be the voice of reason. Be extremely specific about what you want in life and formulate an action plan. Then, maintain consistency and work daily to get closer day by day. Ensure that you are not wasting your time and that you are pushing yourself towards your burning ambitions. Analyse your progress and track your results. For example, if you want to lose weight, set a monthly target to burn the required amount of calories. Then, prepare a strict diet plan and a workout schedule. Track your progress every day by weighing yourself daily.

STAY ORGANISED

Once you've set your goals, you have to organize them properly. What are your long-term goals? What are your short-term goals? Create a schedule and follow it. Plan and organize your sequence of actions, from the time you wake up from bed till you return to sleep. Staying organized will give you a feeling of satisfaction that everything is under control and time is not wasted. It is a feeling of euphoria. However, if you don't organize your day properly, you will end up doing nothing important and in turn, will make you feel low and frustrated.

PRIORITIZE

The Eisenhower Matrix helps us to categorize tasks based upon importance and urgency. This helps us to track how much of our time we manage to utilize properly and how much time we waste on unproductive activities. It helps us to become more productive and selective of how we choose to spend most of our time.

THE EISENHOWER MATRIX

	URGENT	NOT URGENT
IMPORTANT	**DO** DO IT NOW	**DECIDE** SCHEDULE A TIME TO DO THE WORK
NOT IMPORTANT	**DELEGATE** WHO CAN DO IT FOR YOU?	**DELETE** ELIMINATE IT

THE POMODORO

The Pomodoro Technique was developed by Francesco Cirillo in order to manage time effectively and to make optimum use of it. This technique helps you to break down work into intervals with the help of a timer. One pomorodo is equivalent to 25 minutes of undisturbed work and followed by a short break of maybe 5 minutes. Each interval is known as a pomodoro. The point is maximum concentration in that time and reward mechanism. We cannot focus on something for a long duration. Decide on the task to be done. Set the pomodoro timer. Work on the task without any distraction, and when the timer rings stop the task and take a small break to relax yourself. Then repeat the process. This 25-5-25 is the classic method and you can customize it based on your convenience. This technique can help you advance throughout the day without any stress.

Lost time can never be found again. Thus, don't waste even a second and make the utmost use of your time. Spend your time responsibly.

Life is short, time is fast, no replay, no rewind,
so enjoy every moment as it comes.

PAST MISTAKES

Nobody is perfect in this world. Everyone has their flaws in one form or another. All of us would have made a lot of mistakes in the past. There is nothing wrong or odd in making mistakes as it is a natural human tendency to make mistakes. As the saying goes, Mistakes are the stepping stones of success. Your past mistakes are meant to guide you and not define you. Without trial and error, we cannot hope to live our life. We must learn from our mistakes and try not to repeat them when a similar situation arises. They shape and mould us along the way. Only through making mistakes can we expect to learn, grow, mature, and understand life. The issue is that when you fail to accept your past mistakes as a lesson, but remain depressed, you are merely pulling the brakes and holding on to it. By doing so, you are locked in a cycle of guilt, which inhibits further progress. Your past mistakes are meant to guide you in the right path. Don't remind yourself of your past mistakes nor hold on to them, but bear in mind to avoid such crucial mistakes in the future. Don't stress over them as you cannot change anything about it. Sometimes it just takes minutes to forget and move on, while it may take days, months or even years to move on from the mistakes you made. The first-ever thing you must do, is to accept that you made a blunder and that worrying won't change anything. Instead, give yourself a second chance to move on from the mistake. Thus, forgive yourself and don't commit that mistake ever again in your life. It is not so simple to forget and forgive yourself easily if it involves a major debacle. Over time, things change and will become better. However, it will never change overnight. Look back at the problems you faced and the mistakes you made five years ago, and determine their level of importance in your present life. Reassess what you value in your life. Don't live in the past, which adds nothing of value to your life. Learn to live in the present moment you have now. This very moment you are alive, be extremely grateful for that and initiate steps to let go of your past.

When you forgive, you heal
When you let go, you grow

We all make mistakes, and that is completely fine. However, make it a point never to repeat those mistakes over and over again. If you fall, learn to rise up again. Use your past mistakes as a beacon of light. Accept the fact that you cannot travel back to the past and rectify it unless you have a time travel machine. Recognize and realize that every situation will pass. Our problems only seem big because they are our problems. When a friend comes to you with the same problem, we support them by advising that things will turn out all right and eventually settle down. Sometimes, you just need to relax, breathe, and let go. Don't take everything so seriously. What's done is done and belongs to the past. Thus, learn to move on. Life is like a book; some chapters are happy, some are sad, and some are exciting. Don't stay idle and just move on to the next page.

Sometimes you just have to turn the page to realise there is much more in your book of life than the page you may be stuck on. Don't spend your days trying to fix or change your past.
Detach, let go, and start a brand-new page for the next chapter in your life.
-Ricci

THINK OUTSIDE THE BOX

*If you always do **what** you've always done,*
*you'll always get **what** you've always got.*
-Albert Einstein

Don't put yourself in a box and close your box with a big size lid. We self-limit our thinking by our beliefs. The ability to witness things in a way that most people don't basically defines creativity. Strive to break out from your false shell, only then you can truly see what lies outside. The world becomes very narrow if you are close-minded. Thinking outside the box will expand your views, allowing you to attain a greater perspective on your life. You will be more open to different points of view and potential solutions. Thinking outside the box simply means that you are willing to consider different solutions and methods to reach your desired outcome. There are numerous solutions, however our limiting beliefs limit our thoughts within the box.

For example, 2+3=5 is not wrong, but 3+2 also equals 5. You will be surprised to know how interconnected various things are and how it can be dull to reside inside the box. Can you sit inside a room for a month? Thinking inside the box is like sitting inside a boring room. Yes, it is safe and comfortable, but unless you exit the comfort of the room, you will never understand what lies outside. In all aspects of life, approach it from a new perspective or incorporate new ideas. In this manner, you are able to see things from a new and better perspective, only when you think outside the box. As long as your mind expands in different directions, with respect to different aspects, you will never be able to come up with ideas to solve your problem. Thinking differently has a powerful and positive effect. We always think to ourselves that, "You are safer when you are doing what others are doing". Staying as part of a group instead of being left out alone is safe. Deriving inspiration from others is one way to learn. The slang we use, the way we talk, and the way we think is a form of inspiration in one way or the other from other people who you either know personally or whom you admire. When you repeat this process, you become only part of the crowd. If you want to be successful, you have to be different. As quoted by Shiv Khera, "Winners don't do different things, they do things differently." Break out from your shell and come up with different ideas. Maintain clarity in your thoughts and surround yourself with people who encourage you and support you, rather than people who constantly put you down. Whenever an idea springs to your mind, don't hesitate to write it down. More often than not, we think of an idea and assume that we will remember it, which ends up being forgotten. Writing down your ideas can also help you analyse and in turn, provides better clarity. If everyone just accepted things the way they are, then there would be no room for any innovation or improvement in the world. There are numerous possibilities and opportunities outside the box, which can be accessed only if you take the chance to look outside the box. Don't be afraid to be different and stand out of the crowd. Nothing will ever change if you stay within your comfort zone. ***Realize that there is no box and your limiting beliefs create the box.***

Only when you change the way you look at things, the things you look at change.

-Wayne Dyer

DON'T LIVE A LIFE FOR SOCIAL MEDIA

You can still choose to be happy, without other people knowing that you are happy. Every one of us has experienced the feeling of a dopamine rush, when someone provides a positive response on our feed or timeline. The number of likes we receive for each post makes us think we are popular and gives us a sense of pride. We keep scrolling, browsing other profiles as if their lives were more important than ours. Additionally, we tend to compare their life with ours, eventually ending up in depression. We spend hours upon hours editing pictures, to just get meaningless likes from people whom we barely know. To certain individuals, it gives a sense of euphoria. However, when observed carefully, it is an utter waste of time and it spoils our mind with useless junk. What others think of you is not important at all and it is none of your business. What they think of you is from their perception. You don't have any obligations to show how you live your life, what you recently bought or display your financial status to other people.

Nowadays, every single family member tends to stay engrossed in social media; we keep scrolling our phone and the time we spend together is so little. Yes, it connects people and helps us to bring back memories, but it should not eat your time away. Spend your time and energy responsibly.

Observe how much time you spend on social media daily and you will feel guilty when you realise that, you have wasted a lot of time looking at the activities of others. Analyse the time you spend daily on social media and attempt to reduce it as much as possible.

If you spend around 5 hrs average on social media for a day, cut it down to 1 hr a day and you will have an additional 4 hours a day, 28 extra hours a week, 120 hours a month, and 1440 hours a year. This amounts to 60 days extra, which means you have two more extra months a year. Think about how much time you let go to waste and what you could have achieved in that time frame. I know it can be quite difficult to cut down our time spent online immediately. Yes, it can be addictive and tempting to scroll down the feed. However, it is not an impossible feat. You will notice an immediate difference in your routine; you will be more productive without letting your mind get corrupted and influenced by social media. When there is no one to compare to and when there is no one to give you a temporary dopamine charge, you will discover what truly makes you happy. Living a life just to impress others and to get attention is wasting your life. Live your life for yourself. Be yourself. You don't require approval from people for everything you do. Don't live a fake life just to satisfy the people around you and to stay relevant.

SOCIAL MEDIA OFF EXPERIMENT

Log out from your social media for about three weeks. Disconnecting from social media connects you to the actual and real world. You will start to notice,

- You have a lot of time and you can utilise it doing something productive and useful.
- You will get to know yourself better and you will discover a better version of you.
- You will not be influenced or infected by others' opinions. Your peace of mind is undisturbed.
- All the noises saying what you can do and what you can't do will be muted.

- You don't have to constantly communicate or share what you are doing, what you plan on doing, and what you have done.

Instead of scrolling through your social media feed, you can read books and listen to people narrating their life experiences, achievements, failures, etc. This will help you to learn and grow in your life rather than wasting time on useless junk for hours.

SUICIDE IS NOT THE SOLUTION

Suicide does not end the pain,
It just passes it on to someone else.

Most of us would have had the thought of, "I just want to go to sleep and never wake up", at least once in our lifetime. On rare occasions, people take the hasty decision to end their lives over simple issues. They think suicide is the solution to escape reality and to put an end to their problems. When someone you know and care about commits suicide, it is the most heart-breaking experience ever. A culmination of multiple factors drives a person to decide to end their own life.

DEPRESSION

Depression is the primary reason for suicidal thoughts. The cause of depression can be due to anything such as scoring low grades in exams, losing a job, loneliness, hopelessness, bullying, and so on. It varies from person to person. Whatever your problem may be, vent it out immediately and seek help if needed. Avoid mounting pressure within you. Most people who take the extreme step to end their life, are mostly introverts, who choose to dump their feelings and emotions within them. You have to let out your emotions and it is essential to share your problems with someone whom you trust and cares for you. It may be your close friend, your parents or even your siblings. In general, people usually don't discuss suicidal thoughts, fearing that talking about it may only aggravate the situation or make others upset. You will feel light when you share your thoughts with someone.

A problem shared, is a problem halved.

Don't take life very seriously. We are just a minuscule dot in this universe. Everyone has their own problems and not everyone is perfect. If you feel like someone is lonely or depressed, go and talk to them. It's okay if you don't wish to talk, but avoid making fun of them. It is impossible to understand what a person is going through. So, please stop bullying people and teasing them. To you, it may feel like 5 minutes of fun and laughter. However, the same can't be said for the individual playing the victim role. You may mean it in a friendly manner with no ill-intentions, but coping with bullying and teasing is an unpleasant experience.

STRESS

When you hold onto conflicting thoughts in your mind about the same subject, you end up stressed. I want that, but I cannot have it, this creates disharmony in mind and gives rise to stressful emotions. When an opposite thought contradicts a desire you yearn for, either alter the thought or let go of the desire. You can't travel on both paths at the same time. You must pick one.

When someone you are well acquainted with is either depressed or lonely and tells you that they feel like disappearing, please make an effort to go and talk to them. When people feel they have lost all hope, give them hope. You can't hope to see what a person is feeling on the inside. Thus,

- Initiate a conversation with that person.
- Listen to them and show your support.
- Most of the time, all they need is someone to talk to about the problem and someone who would listen to them selflessly without judging.
- Assure the person that you are with them and you are here to help them and gain their trust.
- Cheer them up.

- Take them for a walk.
- Ask them about the reason behind their thought and try to help with finding a solution to their problem.
- Spend time with them and talk to them in a reassuring tone.
- Acknowledge their feelings without judging.
- Support and encourage them to live their life.
- Don't leave them alone and check on them as often as you can.
- Talk to them on a regular basis.
- Keep them busy and engaged. Engaging in specific activities can distract them from such thoughts.
- If they are feeling lost, help them with a plan or a schedule.
- Make them feel, YOU MATTER AND KNOW YOUR WORTH.
- Ask them to appreciate and enjoy life.
- Writing their problems makes it easy. Make a list of the problems they have and try to provide solutions for the problems. Write down the reasons to live and all that they appreciate in life, like the names of people they care for, past happy memories, and positive experiences.
- Make them understand how their loss can affect their near and dear ones and how upset they will be if they are not there.
- You can also encourage them to seek help from a professional.

When you enter a room, you have the power to colour the room with positivity. You can change the vibe, energy, and mood of the people around you. Try your best to keep the people around you happy and always spread good vibes.

If YOU feel like ending your life and you have lost all your hopes,

Calm your mind down
Cease all your thoughts
Just breathe and let go of your thoughts
You have come so far in your life; you have faced all the problems of your past and you can survive the future too.
You will definitely find a solution for your problem, it will come to you, if it does not come it doesn't matter.
No problem is worth ending your life

Most of our problems exist only in our head. We fear for unnecessary things, creating WHAT IF questions such as, what if this happens and that happens. The mere thought of losing someone or something is more dangerous than the actual loss itself. Firstly, clear your mind. Find someone who you can trust and share your problem with and who can help you out. Don't attempt to suppress it within you. Vent it out to someone you trust. Everyone has their problems; some are bigger than yours too, so don't worry. If you still feel like thoughts of suicide persist despite these efforts, do not hesitate to seek help with a mental health expert.

Suicide is a permanent solution to a temporary problem.
- Phil Donahue

EVERYTHING HAPPENS FOR A REASON

"Whatever happened, happened for the good.
Whatever is happening, is happening for the good.
Whatever will happen, will also happen for the good."
-Bhagavad Gita

Let it be good or bad; everything happens for a reason in your life. It may be your time of birth, your zodiac, or karma. Your entire life is scripted the moment you were born. It is already written in the stars and you are merely acting according to that script. As Paramahamsa Yoganandha said, "A divine universal plan exists and…it is beautiful and full of joy". However, you cannot always expect life to be a bed of roses or a cakewalk. If you are going through a bad time, just remember that everything is part of human life. Eventually over time as the weeks, months, and years pass by, everything will be alright. Without these experiences of failure or worry, you would not know what life is. If everything is good in your life, you won't know how to live your life the right way. You will understand what emotions are and the difference between good and bad without those mistakes. Everyone is forced to experience this and you were placed in this situation for a reason, as it prepares you for a bigger, brighter future and to shape you into a better person.

Man cannot remake himself without suffering, for he is both the marble and the sculptor
-Alexis Carrel

You cannot have the pleasure of success without suffering through the pain. It is the law of the universe. Everything will happen as it should happen and sometimes you can do nothing about it, but experience it or just sit back and watch it happening just like a movie. Accept and realize that not everything is under your control. You cannot control everything that happens to you in life. However, you can control how you react and respond.

*Life is 10% what happens to you and 90%
how you react to it.*
-Charles R. Swindoll

Appreciate, recognize, and enjoy the little things of life

*Happiness will never come to those who fail to appreciate
what they already have*
- Buddha

As the day passes by, we fail to notice and appreciate the simple and little things which bring us joy. For example, we wake up in the morning and start our day with a cup of coffee. The question is, have you ever enjoyed your morning coffee to the fullest? The coffee you drink each day has travelled a long journey to arrive in your cup. It has been planted, harvested, processed, dried, roasted, and brewed. All these are processes involved just for your cup of morning coffee. To be more specific, every coffee seed has your name in it. These are the series of events that occur just for your morning cup of coffee. When the coffee is placed on your table, enjoy every sip of it and realise that a lot has been done just for that one cup of coffee. Gratitude is one of the biggest keys to being happy and experiencing joy in your life. When you take a seat at the table for your meal, don't think about what you ate yesterday, what you are going to eat tomorrow or about work. Live in the present moment, don't rush things, be mindful, and enjoy each and every morsel of your food. Try to apply this in every part of your day and you can see noticeable changes in your life. Let things run its course, just enjoy this present moment.

Be in the now, go with the flow, and enjoy whatever comes.

STOP CARING ABOUT WHAT OTHERS THINK

Don't let the noise of others opinions drown out your own inner voice.

-Steve jobs

Most of the time, we lose ourselves and our originality by thinking about what others might think of us and how they would judge us, thus immediately falling into our own trap. You have only one life. Life is too short to waste time waiting for others approval on how you live it. Do not let the opinion of others consume you. Yes, it feels bad when people talk negatively about you. However, your self-worth does not rely on others' opinion of you. When people put us down or talk behind our backs, it does not mean that our life is meaningless or that we are less important. The sooner we ignore these people, the sooner we can stop worrying about what others think of us. At the end of the day, the only thing that matters is what you do and if it makes you happy. It is not easy to overcome the distractions and move on every day in life. Make a conscious decision at this very moment, that your life means more than others' opinions of you and remind yourself that you will not worry about it anymore. It is not worth the hassle nor at the expense of your mental health. Just keep doing what you have to do and move forward. Everything else will eventually fall into place over time.

I AM NOT WHAT I THINK I AM
I AM NOT WHAT YOU THINK I AM
I AM WHAT I THINK YOU THINK I AM

-Charles Cooley

You are here to live your life and not to make everyone understand. You are not a tub of ice cream to make everyone happy. There will be people who praise you and those who talk ill behind your back. Do not take anything to heart. Everyone has a different perception and a different view of life. Just keep doing what makes you happy. If no one were there to judge you, will you be able to do what you are currently doing? Just enjoy your life and dance like nobody's watching. Be yourself and be happy. Don't live based on others' opinions.

Don't waste your time with explanations,
people only hear what they want to hear.
- Paulo Coelho

Don't give your remote to others

Don't let any external factor control you. The biggest mistake we do is, we allow others to control our mood and the way we feel. We become happy when appreciated and sad when we hear negative remarks about us. Someone can text you halfway around the world and you don't even have to see their face or hear their voice, and they can affect your breathing, heart rate, and make you sweat. They can make your situation better or worse, with just a few words. A simple text message or a call can trigger your emotions and make you happy or sad or angry. Take a moment and think, how people and situations may affect your happiness. Do not allow anyone or anything to control the way you feel. No external factor should determine your level of happiness. Keep your remote control safely with yourself. Remember, only you are responsible for how you feel.

PART THREE

HACK

CHAKRAS

Chakras are the energy centres of the body. There are seven primary chakras located along the spine, starting from the base of the spine and running upwards to the crown of the head.

Muladhara - The Root Chakra
Swadhishthana - The Sacral Chakra
Manipura - The Solar Plexus Chakra
Anahata - The Heart Chakra
Vishuddha - The Throat Chakra
Ajna - The Third Eye Chakra
Sahastrara - The Crown Chakra

These seven primary chakras are the basis of our human existence. Each chakra has its vibrational frequency and it relates to specific spiritual, emotional, psychological, and physical aspects of our being. Blockage or imbalance of these chakras can lead to physical, psychological, and emotional disorders. The entire universe is made of energy and this includes our body as well. Balancing of these energy centers plays an important role in the balance of our bodies. Chakras can get blocked and can cause a lot of problems in your day to day life. These blocks create an imbalance in your mind, body, and soul. Recognizing these energy blocks and healing them requires immense patience. Y**ou can become more in tune with the natural energy cycles of your body and make every cell in your body awaken and rejoice if you know how to balance the chakras.** Here are a few things you can do to open your chakras. These three M's will help you balance your chakras.

Meditation

Meditation is a practice to experience the present moment. It helps you to be present here and now. The real secret of life is to be completely engaged with what you are doing at the present moment. Sadly, we are completely preoccupied with memories and expectations. We do not live in the present moment. When we stop talking to ourselves and stop thinking, we realize that there is only this present moment; the eternal now. A person who is constantly lost in thought has nothing to live for except their thoughts. So, he loses touch with reality and lives in a world of illusion. They fail to live because they are always preparing to live. Don't rush anything. Don't worry about the future. Live happily now in this eternal moment. Life is not a problem to be solved, but a reality to be experienced. Practising meditation helps you to divorce yourself from attachments and experience the present moment. Stop the process of labelling an experience, or forcing logic and reason when there is no need for it. Empty your mind and enter a state of thoughtlessness. Meditation is the most powerful tool for opening your blocked chakras. It is the gateway to the present moment and it helps you to experience reality.

There is no specific way to meditate. There are different methods and techniques. There are all sorts of mantras and breathing techniques as well. But, the only ultimate aim to meditate is to be in the now.

'Getting Into the Meditative State'

The easiest way to get into the meditative state is to begin by listening. Simply close your eyes and allow yourself to hear all the sounds that are going on around you, listen to the general hum and buzz of the world as you listen to music. Don't try to identify the sounds you are hearing, don't put names on them, simply allow them to play with your eardrums. Let them go.

In other words, let your ears hear whatever they want to hear. Don't judge the sounds: there are no proper sounds nor improper sounds, and it doesn't matter if somebody coughs or sneezes or drops something — it's all just sound.

As you pursue that experiment, you will very naturally find that you can't help naming sounds, identifying them, and go thinking, talking to yourself inside your head, automatically. But it's important that you don't try to repress those thoughts by forcing them out of your mind because that will have precisely the same effect as if you were trying to smooth rough water with a flatiron — you're just going to disturb it all the more. What you do is this: as you hear sounds coming into your head, thoughts, you simply listen to them as part of the general noise going on just as you would be listening to cars going by, or birds chattering outside the window. So look at your own thoughts as just noises. And soon you will find that the outside world and the inside world come together. They are happening. Your thoughts are happening just like the sounds going on outside, and everything is simply a happening and all you are doing is watching it.

- Alan Watts

Mudras

Mudras are specific hand positions or physical gestures that have an effect on the energy flow of the body. The positioning of your fingers has some form of influence on the energies of the body and your mood. We practise a lot of mudras without even being aware of them. The "Namaste" greeting gesture, where the hands are held in front of the chest with palms together and fingertips of both hands touching each other and the Christian crossing of the fingers during prayer are also a form of mudras. While in deep thought, some of us bring the tips of all fingers from the right hand, towards the corresponding fingertips from the left, which is known as Hakini mudra. You can practise mudra for a couple of minutes or throughout the day. You can practise these anywhere and at any time. The purpose of mudras is to bring about a complete regeneration and transformation of the body-mind principle and an expansion of the consciousness. Each mudra has its unique benefits. They help to liberate the energy that might be struck and help to open the chakras. Mudras are used to balance the five vital elements of the body, which are earth, water, fire, air, and space. Each finger is associated with one of these elements.

THUMB FINGER - Represents the fire element, connected to the solar plexus chakra.

INDEX FINGER - Represents the air element, connected to the heart chakra.

MIDDLE FINGER - Represents the space element, connected to the throat chakra.

RING FINGER - Represents the earth element, connected to the root chakra.

LITTLE FINGER - Represents the water element, connected to the sacral chakra.

Any defect in these elements can cause disorder and imbalance in the mind and body.

These seven mudras can be used to activate the seven chakras of the body

Prithvi Mudra

This mudra helps in activating the Root Chakra. The root chakra holds the elemental force of vital energy. Some of the benefits of the Prithvi mudra are increased energy, inner stability, and confidence.

Touch the tips of the thumb and ring fingers together and keep the other fingers straight.

Chin Mudra

Chin mudra activates the Ajna Chakra, which is your third eye and it stimulates the brain. It is associated with knowledge and wisdom. It helps to calm you down. It also increases your focus and concentration.

Touch the tips of the thumb and the index fingers together and keep the other three fingers straight.

Prana Mudra

Prana mudra activates the Crown Chakra and allows us to surrender to higher consciousness.

Touch the thumb, ring, and the little finger together and keep the other fingers straight.

Varun Mudra

Varun Mudra activates the Sacral Chakra. It helps to balance the water element of the body.

Touch the tip of the thumb and little finger together and keep the other fingers straight or relaxed.

Apana Mudra

Apana Mudra activates the Manipura Chakra and it helps to detox and cleanse the body and mind.

Touch the tip of the thumb, middle, and ring fingers together and keep the other fingers straight.

Anjali Mudra

Anjali Mudra activates the Heart Chakra. It symbolises a connection with your heart and your inner divine self.

Place the palms together near the heart with a small space in between the palms.

Granthita Mudra

Granthita Mudra activates the Throat Chakra, allowing your communication, voice, and expression to be clearer and more authentic.

Interlace your fingers and touch the thumb and index fingers together, creating two interlocked circles, and hold the hands in front of the base of your throat.

Mantras

A mantra is a sound, word, or phrase that you can chant during meditation. The word *mantra* is derived from two Sanskrit words—*manas* (mind) and *tra* (tool). Mantra literally means a tool for the mind. Mantra is a sound vibration through which we mindfully focus our thoughts and our feelings. The science of mantras is a combination of sound waves and their frequencies through phonetics. Chanting mantras creates a resonance in and around the head. The pronunciation of these specific sounds will create vibrations through lips, tongue, palate, back of the throat, and skull, which results in the release of relaxing hormones and calms the mind. It is the basis of sound healing. Not only mantras but also the words we speak and every sound has a frequency and vibration, which affects the human body. Since 60% of our body is water, it has direct effects from the vibrations of sound. Water changes its structure when exposed to different frequencies. There are different types of mantras. Every mantra activates a particular energy in different parts of the body. ***One such mantra is the gayatri mantra, which is proved to be potent and very powerful.***

The Gayatri Mantra

Om Bhuur-Bhuvah Svah
Tat-Savitur-Varennyam
Bhargo Devasya Dhiimahi
Dhiyo Yo Nah Prachodayaat ||

Vishvamitrar composed the Gayatri mantra. It was first written in the Rig Veda, an early Vedic text. The mantra is a hymn to Savitur, the sun god. There are twenty-four letters in the Gayatri Mantra. These 24 letters are the symbol of twenty-four powers and abilities and each of them is related to a specific deity. Chanting the Gayatri mantra elevates a person's mind and soul to a higher level. The vibrations created by the chanting of this mantra directly works on the three chakras of the body-namely the third eye, throat, and crown chakras. It stimulates the pineal gland, which helps in releasing Endorphins and other relaxing hormones in the body. It keeps the person calm and more focused.

The GAYATRI MANTRA is broadcasted daily for 15 minutes from 7 P.M onwards over Radio Paramaribo, Surinam, South America, Holland, and in Amsterdam.

There are many such mantras. The effects of mantras on the human body is miraculous, yet it is science. They play a very important role in balancing our chakras and to calm the mind. The benefits of chanting mantras should be experimented and experienced.

THE THIRD EYE

The Pineal gland, popularly known as the third eye is the Ajna chakra, it is located between our two physical eyes. It is a tiny pea-sized endocrine gland situated alone in the centre of the brain between the two hemispheres. The pineal gland is described as "the principal seat of the soul" and the portal to the higher dimensions. Under the microscope, it is made up of cells that share the same features as the rod-shaped light-sensitive cells found in our retinas. It produces melatonin and regulates our daily circadian rhythm, regulates our sleep and wake cycle, and the quality of our sleep. Serotonin, the neurotransmitter or happy chemical responsible for our mood is transformed into melatonin only in the pineal gland. This is the site where the brain regulates consciousness and interprets the sensory and motor functions of our body. The Pineal Gland plays an essential role in physical, mental and spiritual well-being and is a gateway to higher consciousness. When the pineal gland is not functioning at its optimum level, we are often not even aware of a problem existing. A blocked Ajna chakra leads to confusion, uncertainty, jealousy, and ego. A simple way of activating the third eye is through meditation, especially meditating with your focus between your eyebrows. When the third eye is open and active, a gentle pressure can be felt between our eyebrows, through which we can experience clarity of thought and become more intuitive.

The pineal gland gets calcified or blocked due to exposure of toxins in the environment. In general, we are exposed to a higher range of chemicals, through the air we breathe, the water we drink, and the food we consume. The Pineal Gland is very sensitive to chemicals. Calcification of the pineal gland can lead to confusion and mental clouding. In addition, the

Pineal gland is very sensitive to fluoride in tap water and gets calcified and blocked. Fluoride is likely to cause decreased melatonin production and affects the normal function of the pineal gland. Preservatives and chemicals in food also affect the pineal gland. It is important to detox the body in order to decalcify the pineal gland. Lifestyle changes such as drinking pure water and using fluoride-free toothpaste, limiting the intake of sugar, caffeine, alcohol, and consuming natural fresh food free from preservatives can help in decalcification of the pineal gland.

When your mind is clear and your third eye is open, you can see and know things that are taking place thousands of miles away from you.

-Frederick Lenz

LAW OF ATTRACTION

Ask, and it will be given to you;
Seek, and you will find;
Knock, and the door will be opened to you.
- *Matthew 7:7*

The Law of Attraction states that you will attract into your life whatever you focus on. It is the most powerful law in the universe. It persists in your life at this very moment. You are always in a state of creation. You are making steps to creating your reality in every moment. You are creating your future with every single thought, either consciously or subconsciously. Whatever you give your energy and attention to, will come back to you. We are what we think we are. Thus, if you stay focused on the good and positive things in your life, you will automatically attract good and positive things into your life. If you constantly stay focused on negativity, then you will only invite negative aspects into your life. Wrong thoughts attract unwanted emotions and events into your life. Your thoughts and feelings are responsible for the events taking place around you.

Your thought determines everything that comes into your life and everything that you experience. It is our thoughts that shape our lives and the world around us. Every thought is made up of energy and has its own unique frequency. When this energy and frequency of a single thought radiates out into the Universe, it naturally interacts with the material world. As your thought radiates out, it attracts the energy and frequencies of like thoughts, like objects, and even like people, in turn drawing them back to you. During every second of our existence, either knowingly or unknowingly, we act as human magnets sending out and attracting back energies. This is the Law of Attraction.

Everything is energy and that's all there is to it. Match the frequency of the reality you want and you cannot help but get that reality. It can be no other way. This is not philosophy. This is physics.
– Albert Einstein

We are like artists painting on a blank canvas. The colours you use are your thoughts and the canvas is your reality. We are able to shape our reality with our thoughts. You can paint whatever you want on the blank canvas. Regardless of if you trust in God or are an atheist, we all accept the fact that there exists a power above us which allows things to function. Even the prayers to God are based on the law of attraction. Your thoughts are very powerful. Every single thought you think today, feelings you feel today, and the actions you take today will determine your experience tomorrow. Your thoughts tailor you. Your entire reality is all within your head. You are consciously creating your reality with every thought. The colours you see and the sounds you hear are nothing but vibrations. Everything is a form of vibration. The entire process occurs on the inside, within our minds. Once we discover how to condition our minds to our desired frequencies of vibration, our reality changes. When you drop a pen, it falls on the ground; it is the law of gravity. Likewise, whatever you think constantly and ask the universe will manifest, which is the law of attraction. It is the law and you cannot change it. It is a universal principle. The better you understand it, the more you can start predicting and expect what happens to you. Your awareness of the Law of Attraction can change your whole life.

DECIDE WHAT YOU WANT

Realize that this is your moment; your time to begin consciously, intentionally, and deliberately participating in the creation of the future you desire. Most of us roam around arbitrarily without any intentions. We wake up, make preparations, and proceed to our routine work daily. In this manner, we complete the entire day aimlessly wandering.

We get distracted by unwanted thoughts and feelings and we drift away from our goal. The first thing you have to do to achieve your desired life is to be intentional and set your goal. Be specific about what you want in your life.

VISION BOARD

Create a vision board with pictures of what you want to attract your way and how your life should be. Attach pictures of what all you want to achieve in your life; it provides you clarity. Visualise it and invest energy towards making it real. The images on your vision board will remind you of your desires. Place the board where you spend most of your time and look at it as often as you can, so that you can begin working towards it.

THE ART OF ASKING

Ask the Universe what you want and not what you don't want. What you think about, talk about, and give your attention to will manifest. Every minute, you are sending requests to the universe and your subconscious mind by your thoughts. Be more deliberate about what you think and feel. Focus on and talk about what you want. The more you think about it, the faster you will manifest your dreams. Picture yourself achieving it and celebrating it and thanking the universe for giving you what you asked for. Do not doubt or think about how it will manifest or how it is possible. The hardest part of building or breaking any habit is that initial attempt. It gets considerably easier after that. Your neural pathways are rewired and you start thinking and behaving differently. It moves from the conscious mind to the subconscious mind. Ask the universe for whatever you want. Eventually, you will begin to realize that what you are doing now and everything that you have now is a result of what you wished.

BELIEVE THE PROCESS

Don't have any doubts and have faith in the process. Set a time period. Nothing ever changes overnight, but firmly believe that it will happen and work towards it. Sweep away all your doubts. Most people limit their belief about their dreams. You must make efforts to change such beliefs and be confident that you are good enough, smart enough, strong enough, attractive enough, rich enough then you think you are, and capable of achieving whatever you want in your life. Possess a strong belief that the universe can make it happen for you. Once you believe that you can achieve whatever you desire and take actions every day towards your goal and purpose, it will manifest automatically.

EXPERIENCE IT NOW

How happy will you feel if you have manifested everything you asked for and achieved your goal? Practice feeling the emotions you would be experiencing as if you already have what you wanted and what you asked for.

Close your eyes and visualize what you want. Assume you are imagining your dream car. Close your eyes and visualize the car in your mind. Picture it as clearly as you can. Visualize every detail as if it were before you. Imagine yourself holding the steering wheel and feel it in your hands. Feel the cosy leather seats and feel its texture. Breathe in deeply and smell the cabin of your car. Listen and enjoy the acoustic sound your car makes when you start the engine. Visualize yourself shifting the gear and throttling. Experience how it feels to drive your dream car. This is called sensory visualization. Experience those emotions through your thoughts as if you already have accomplished it. It is similar to "fake it until you make it."

PATIENCE

Rome wasn't built in a day,
but they were laying bricks every hour.
-John Heywood

We want whatever we desire and are impatient in most cases. You cannot sow a seed tonight, water it, and expect a tree the very next day. We lack patience and we start worrying that things won't happen overnight as they take time. We have to realise that anything in life that is worthwhile will never come easy. Those sleepless nights, times spent on your work, the constant never-ending desire, and hard work to achieve your goal will eventually be worthwhile. Everything will manifest gradually. All you need to practice is to trust the process and be patient.

You are the author of your life story. You have the power to create the type of life you want. You are the designer of your own world.

What you think you become.
What you feel you attract.
What you imagine you create.
– Buddha

SOUND HEALING

Sound healing or music therapy is the concept of using vibrations to relax your mind and body. The entire Universe is in a state of vibration. It may be anything from the humming of birds in the morning to your favourite rock metal band. Every sound you hear has an effect on you. The human body comprises about 60 percent water. Water changes its structure when it is exposed to sound or a particular frequency. This is termed water cymatics. So, every sound has an effect on you. Even the beating of your heart and your voice is a form of vibration. The basic principle of sound healing is the concept of vibratory frequency. When sound waves reach our ears, they get converted into neurological signals, through the auditory nerve into the auditory cortex of the brain and then it is processed. Every sound you hear can alter your brain waves. Music is believed to connect the physical, emotional, and spiritual realms simultaneously. That is why listening to your favourite music can change your mood instantly.

Music can change the world.
- Beethoven

Sound healing synchronizes brain waves to achieve profound states of relaxation, helping to restore the normal vibratory frequencies of the cells in our bodies. It has also been used to treat a number of conditions such as depression, anxiety, autism, and post-traumatic stress disorder.

Our brain has five different types of brain waves. Each of these brain waves has a normal frequency range.

Frequency range	Name	Usually associated with:
> 40 Hz	Gamma waves	Higher mental activity, including perception, problem-solving, and consciousness
13–39 Hz	Beta waves	Active, busy thinking, active processing, active concentration, arousal, and cognition
7–13 Hz	Alpha waves	Calm relaxed yet alert state
4–7 Hz	Theta waves	Deep meditation /relaxation, REM sleep
< 4 Hz	Delta waves	A deep dreamless sleep, loss of body awareness

Each type of brainwave controls different states of consciousness. The dominant brain wave will determine your current state of mind. Everything happening in our daily lives can disturb the balance of our brain waves. You can manually set your desired state of mind by tuning into a particular mode by certain ways similar to tuning a radio channel. Your mind is the receiver and you just need to tune in with the universe.

There are a few different types of sound therapy,

SOLFEGGIO FREQUENCIES

Listening to music or any sound at a particular frequency can heal you. Specific sound patterns are used to change your state of mind by altering your brain waves. Nikola Tesla, *one of the greatest* and yet less understood inventors of all times said , “If we can control that resonate system electronically, we can directly control the entire mental system of humankind”.

The Tesla Code 369 is called the magic frequency. The Solfeggio Frequencies include a set of sacred numbers with a repeating sequence of 3, 6 and 9, and each Solfeggio Frequency has a specific purpose.

If you want to find the secrets of the universe, think in terms of energy, frequency, and vibration.
If you only knew the magnificence of the 3, 6, and 9, then you would have a key to the universe.
- Nikola Tesla.

These tones contain the frequency required to balance your energy and heal you. The commonly used Solfeggio Frequencies are:

174 Hz – Removes Pain
396 Hz – Liberates Guilt and Fear
417 Hz – Facilitates Change
432Hz – Clarity of thought
528 Hz – Transformation and Miracles
639 Hz – Heals Relationships
741 Hz – Awakens Intuition
852 Hz – Returning to Spiritual Order
963 Hz – Divine Consciousness or Enlightenment

From my personal experience, listening to 432 Hz can instantly change your state of mind and provide clarity. Mozart and Verdi employed 432 Hz for all of their music. It is called the miracle tone and is the natural frequency of the universe.

BINAURAL BEATS

When you hear two tones, one in each ear, that are slightly different in frequency, your brain processes a beat at the difference of the frequencies. If you listen to a tone of 200 Hz in your left ear and a tone of 205 Hz in your right ear, your brain will automatically perceive an illusory tone and produce a new frequency of 5 Hz (205 – 200 = 5 Hz). This third tone is called a binaural beat. It is a frequency following response where the brain automatically aligns the brainwaves to this frequency and allows you to change your state of mind as desired. Put on your headphones, decide which frequency range, and find a comfortable place free from distractions. Now you can manually tune your brain waves.

*All types of binaural beats and solfeggio frequencies are available online.

VOCAL TONING

The most basic musical instrument you can use is your voice. You can use your voice by humming, chanting or singing. That is why many mantras are so powerful. Some specific tones and words can alter your state of mind. Vocal toning uses seven tones based on vowels. Each one is connected to a particular chakra of the body.

CHAKRA	SOUND
MULADHARA	UH
SVADISTHANA	OOO
MANIPURA	OH
ANAHATA	AH
VISHUDHA	EYE
AJNA	AYE
SAHASHARA	EEE

TUNING FORKS

Tuning forks, when calibrated at a particular frequency, can be held to specific parts of the body to send vibrations that release tension and open blocked energy channels.

SINGING BOWLS

Singing bowls have been used in Tibetan culture since the 12th century. As each bowl produces a unique vibration that works on separate parts of the brain, bowls of various sizes are often used together.

GONGS

Gongs and bells can be seen in most temples. They produce vibrations that work on the mind-body connection. The sound produced by a gong can send you into a deeply relaxed and meditative state in as quickly as 60 to 90 seconds.

Music can heal wounds, that medicine cannot touch.
Sound will be the medicine of the future.
-Edgar Cayce

11: 11

When you check the time on the clock, it is 11:11 am. A sharp chill runs through your spine. Deep down, you intuitively sense that this number has some form of great importance. In actuality, you don't know what it means. If you have been seeing 11: 11 and other repetitive numbers sequences such as 111, 222, 333, 444, 555, there lies an important reason as to why you're seeing these numbers more often. These numbers are wake up calls for your Soul from the Universe. Many people believe that seeing the numbers 11: 11 signifies that your spirit guides are attempting to contact you. Numbers are the language of the universe. The universe communicates to you only through numbers and certain signs. It is just a number when you do not understand nor recognise it. It is a concept of synchronicity and metaphysical encounter leading to a sense of wonder and intuition. All numbers have different vibrational properties. According to numerology, everything can be calculated such as birth dates, names, and places to discover deep hidden truths. The number 11 is like a "master number", which signifies intuition, insight, and spiritual enlightenment. In my personal experience, the number 11: 11 seems to signify that you are on the right path, your actions are aligned with the purpose of your soul, and you are being assisted by your spirit guides and the universe. It is a clear message from the universe. Seeing 11:11 is a beautiful reminder that you are aligned and being guided. You may see this number on number plates, clocks, bills, and just about anywhere. Pay attention when you see it; be aware and remember to stay grounded in the present moment. When you see numbers such as 11:11 more often, you are present in the divine flow of life. It can be quite difficult to explain, but unless you possess first-hand experience, it will be impossible to comprehend. It is similar to asking someone to show the air that you breathe, which can only be felt as a breeze. You will notice something happening beyond the veil of physical reality. You might be confused on deciding something and for no particular reason, you check the time on the screen, which coincidentally happens to be 11:11. Witnessing these number sequences repeatedly is a sign that you are in sync with the universe and you are receiving a form of intuitive guidance or support from your spirit guides. It is a very powerful moment in which your intentions will manifest with a degree of speed and efficiency never before experienced. Some say that the numbers 11 11 signals a spiritual presence, while some argue that seeing 11:11 is an auspicious sign, with the numbers themselves having mystical powers. It would seem that the more you start to notice these events, the more often it appears to show up in your life.

When you see these number sequences, the first thing you should do is stop for a moment and become aware of your thoughts or actions you are engaged in at that very time. Be completely aware of your current surroundings, such as the thoughts, the voice in your head, the song playing or who you are talking to, and what you are about to do.

Numbers carry their own specific and unique vibration, which you can use to decipher the message the universe may be trying to communicate to you based on the number sequences you are seeing.

000: New beginnings. A fresh start. Being one with the Universe. A reminder that you are the creator of your own destiny.

111: Your intentions are manifesting quickly. Make sure you're focusing on what you actually WANT, not what you don't want.

222: Stop worrying. Everything is working out just as it is supposed to. Trust that you are on the right path.

333: The ascended masters are right by you, assisting you with whatever it is that you're currently working on. You're in great hands.

444: You are completely surrounded by angels. You are being guided through whatever you are focusing on. Enjoy the process.

555: Big changes are up ahead. Trust that this transition is your highest good. Prepare for massive shifts. Things are getting exciting.

666: Your thoughts require some refocusing. This is a reminder that you are a spiritual being having a human experience. Reconnect with your spirituality.

777: Luck is on your side. You are on the ultimate spiritual path. Keep doing what you're doing. You already contain the wisdom you need.

888: You are the authority of your own life. Financial abundance is on its way to you right now. You are aligned with the money you desire.

999: You are being encouraged to finish something because that completion will unlock the next step for you. Effortlessly release what no longer serves you and prepare for what actually brings you peace.

1111: You are on the right path. You're a master manifestor and know exactly where you're heading. Alignment at its finest.

The next time you see a recurring number code, see if the numerological energy aligns with what you are feeling.

ABOUT THE AUTHOR

The author Arjun Karthik, is a twenty-three-year-old Doctor from Salem, India. He was always passionate in the field of Psychology and Human behaviour. Over the last few years, he would often focus on how people reacted to different scenarios. Arjun possesses a burning passion for understanding people, helping them uncover their true potential, and to make them know their worth.

Email id - mvarjunkarthik@gmail.com
Instagram - quark_1111